Like a Chinook—both a wind and the salmon—her art almost levitates from home streams where she has anchored herself. Ann Fox Chandonnet shapes us an enormous cut bank with her river of words. She is a storyteller, as each poem is a chrysalis in her narrative. I feel cool gravel beds where my life as a reader galvanizes onto hers.

Ann's attention to life encapsulations is the bedrock of her anadromous words. More than a hundred poems are celebratory as well as incantations for people, places, pathways taken. From the shape of her birth in Lowell, Mass., to her home haunts in Chugiak, Anchorage, and Juneau, Alaska, to her residence in Vale, North Carolina, and now in Lake St. Louis, Missouri, Ann is the definition of "wordsmith," as she's honed her ear and mind's eye to revel in humanity and Earth.

Her poetry is trawled from a multilayered observer of life, as she's been a wife, teacher, mother, newspaper reporter, food historian, non-fiction book author, and poet. She collaborates with so many muses and historical narratives in this long collection. Yet, her voice is a mercurial shape of wind on water.

—Paul K. Haeder, essayist, educator, and author of the story collection
Wide Open Eyes: Surfacing from Vietnam (Cirque), Oregon

Ann Fox Chandonnet's sublime and varied poetry aptly describes a vast landscape of emotion. She takes us along as she travels the bumpy road of menopause with raw outbursts of rage, grief, and frustration in "Estrogen: A Letter":

"...now I glimpse your slimy hidden agenda:
You set me up for a really big fall.
In the autumn of my life,
You skedaddled under cover of darkness,
Pruning my vocabulary like an apple sucker.
Tongue-tied, stumbling,
I suspected as much.
But now medical research confirms it."

In another poem, "The Final Approach," we witness the nightmarish tragedy of 9/11 as it is glimpsed from the pilot's viewpoint, his plane smashing into the North Tower. The story behind this poem is that the pilot was a family friend and farmer. So, the scene embraces a personal grief and imagery.

It could be true that Ann Chandonnet's genius has been pared by the passage of time and menopause. What is left, however, is astonishingly full and exquisite. More than enough. Would that all who aspire to bring magic to the reader be as eloquent.

—Teresa Ascone, watercolor artist, fabric designer, author, and potter, Anchorage, Alaska.

THE SHAPE OF WIND ON WATER

NEW AND SELECTED POEMS

THE SHAPE OF WIND ON WATER

NEW AND SELECTED POEMS

ANN FOX CHANDONNET

LP

Loom Press
Amesbury, Massachusetts
2023

The Shape of Wind on Water: New and Selected Poems

ISBN 978-0-931507-52-6

Published in the United States of America
First Edition

Design: Keith Finch
Font: Bebas Neue, Futura, and Garamond Premier
Cover photograph: Steve Dieffenbacher
Author photograph: Tim Parker
Printing: Versa Press, Illinois

Some poems in the New section were published in *Abraxas 49, Alaska Quarterly Review, Archipelago, Cirque Journal, Etcetera, Gaia, Harpoon, Hawk & Whippoorwill, Ice-Floe, Kaldron, Kalliope, Kansas Quarterly, Minotaur, Mr. Cogito, Northeast Journal, Northward Journal, Orca, permafrost, Sin Fronteras, Slant, Stella Borealis, Sun-Catcher: Children of the Earth, The Dead Mule School of Poetry, The Great Lander, The Lowell Review, The Outer Coast Calendar, We Alaskans* (Anchorage *Daily News* magazine), and *Wild Goose.*

Several poems appeared in anthologies: *Black Sun, New Moon*; *Dogs Singing*; *Innisfree*; *Last New Land*; *When Last on the Mountain*; *Sun-Catcher: Children of Earth*; *The Sky's Own Light*; *In the Dreamlight*; and *Whispered Secrets.*

"See and Release" won the Utah Wilderness Society's Poetry Contest, 1990. "Learning Eskimo Dancing/ Lighting Up the World," is included in Ruggero Maggi's Shadow Project Archive in Milan, Italy, a 1991 anti-war project with visual and literary works from more than 300 artists in 38 countries.

Loom Press
15 Atlantic View, Amesbury, MA 01913
www.loompress.com
info@loompress.com

Also by Ann Fox Chandonnet

Incunabula (1968)
At the Fruit-Tree's Mossy Root: The Marsh Hill Idylls (1968, 1980)
The Complete Fruit Cookbook (1972)
The Wife & Other Poems (1976)
The Wife: Part Two (1979)
Ptarmigan Valley: Poems of Alaska (1980)
Auras, Tendrils (1984)
Chief Stephen's Parky: A Year in the Life of an Athabascan Girl (1989)
Canoeing in the Rain (1990)
The Alaska Heritage Seafood Cookbook (1995, 2021)
Gold Rush Grub: From Turpentine Stew to Hoochinoo (2005)
Alaska's Inside Passage (2006; second edition 2009)
"Write Quick!": War and a Woman's Life in Letters, 1835-1867 (2010)
Colonial Food (2013)
Barn Raisings and Cemetery Cleanings:
An American Celebrations Cookbook (2016)
Baby Abe: A Lullaby for Lincoln (2021)

“I knew I could not pull a curtain
on the past, so I wear it.”

—Shelby Stephenson, via email, 12/11/2022

Contents

NEW

People

Snow Water under Culverts 5
My Muse 9
Fur-Face 10
Gross Anatomy 101 13
One Nest, One Burrow 14
The Civil War Ink Bottle 17
In the Horse 19
Fine Shining Weather: Three Poems for John Muir 21
Iris is Last 29
The Translator's Grandson 31
Learning Eskimo Dancing/Lighting Up the World 32
Kissing the Frog 36
A Baby Walks 37

Places

Sitka 41
Cogs Within Cogs 43
It Pushes 46
Under Mendenhall 47
Brash Ice (Auke Lake, Juneau, Alaska) 48
See and Release 50
Gold Creek, Ouzel 51
Words for Shadows 52
Circle of Stones 54
Near Greenwood (Tulsa), 1921 55
The Effect of Recorded Hymns on White Tails 57

Fireflies in Amish Country 58
Borning Room 60
The Final Approach 61
Buzzard Song 62
The Hare in Tuckerman's Ravine 63
First Words 66
Willendorf, Early June 67
At Max Yasgur's Farm, 1969 (Woodstock) 74
Maui Sunset 75

Correspondence

The Poet as the Letter P: Stevens Requests More Prunes 79
A Postcard from Sandburg's Cellar 81
Estrogen: A Letter 84
Peavey: A Letter 86

Harvest

One Summer before 1950 91
Whalescape 92
September 15, 12:04 p.m. 95
Shooting Down New Year 96
Owl Chuck (Anchorage) 97
Now Desire 99
Understanding the Oedipus Complex 101
Sides-to-the-Middle 103
Subdivisions 105
The House That Bias Built 106
Driving Black 108
Mary Porter is Carried from the Morning Star Baptist Church in Mattapan 110
Howl for Edo 113

SELECTED POEMS

The Wife & Other Poems (1976)
The Wife ... 121
Aubade in International Orange ... 123
Gram: Only the Ashes ... 124
Love in Mother Lode Country ... 132
Adoption ... 133
The Island ... 135

The Wife: Part 2 (1979)
Notes on Speech ... 139
Hard Candy ... 142
Building a Fire in the Rain ... 144

Ptarmigan Valley: Poems of Alaska (1980)
Van Cliburn Among the Crowberries ... 149
Ptarmigan Valley ... 150
The Walrus Come to Gambell in the Spring ... 151
Sonatina: Inukshuk ... 152
Woods (Lowell) ... 153
On a Human Scale ... 154
Grizzly ... 155
Trapper ... 156
The Ermine ... 157
Allego ... 158

At the Fruit-Tree's Mossy Root (1968, 1980)
The Underground ... 163
Peas ... 165
Voice Lessons ... 166
Laurel ... 169
The Barn in Winter ... 171

Auras, Tendrils (1984)
Entering the Surroundings 175
Masks 176
Auras, Tendrils 177
In Velvet 178

Canoeing in the Rain (1990)
Into the Realm of the Seal 187
Aleut Lullaby 489
How Little Children Come to Suffer 191
Side Spike 194

The Octopus: An Essay 195

Notes 201
A Note on the Author 207

NEW

People

Snow Water Under Culverts

—The title is from a poem by Louise Bogan.

When asked about "the disappeared" of Guatemala, an army officer of that country told the National Public Radio interviewer, "They like to travel, and then they come back in the country under different names."

Everything is hard, gray, frozen here,
but in his country snow water trickles in culverts,
caching bits of bone swept from the fields,
nutrients hard won—
the first scent of spring (wet dirt),
and the tooth-numbing, palm-tingling ditch draught,
spicules of ice in it still,
refreshing as a McIntosh.

The scent of new pine boards,
fresh cement,
manure of several species,
scalded steel and sour milk in the milk room,
ripening silage forked down the hemispherical ladder shaft
(like ascending into a mine),
moldering hay in the high mows.

These all come flooding back,
these bits of a rural childhood:
acrid fug of bald rubber, lugs, trickles of solder,
the five o'clock shadow of quinces,
stuttering arc light glimpsed through dirty shop windows,
the Masonic emblem Dad covertly welded on machinery
brought from neighboring farms for repairs.

The past loops and knots,
falls in coils like heavy rope,
like steaming umbilical cord—
fastening to an unborn calf's legs and pulling,
fastening to a section of silo roof and pulling,
hauling bricks in a bucket for the shop chimney,
tying up bales the baler skipped,
circling.

When hernia tied him to a blue chair
(a chair he had carpentered),
I was stunned, puzzled:
he never sat still during daylight hours except to eat.
Stilled, he stopped the universe.

I kept returning to that padded chair on the sun porch,
circling his motionless feet,
waiting for news of normality.
(The figurative turned away at the door;
Mom's Monet prints banished to the attic.)

He brought us a nest of wild rabbits
who slept in a grapefruit crate in the kitchen,
crows who gobbled bread sopped in milk
and were disgusting diners,
three raccoons, a fine squirrel.

When he could afford them
wrapped gifts in the funny papers—
both for thrift's sake and because real gift wrap seemed sentimental, coy.
Once gave us light fixtures,
the cheap dishes needed to modernize.
The dining room fixture was mine.
(Later denied this,
embarrassed at poverty's indignities.)

Not a home of conversation,
but of silent Mayflowers, companionable crickets,
frogs, tractors, tedders, conveyor belts,
disc harrows, flies, apples rumbling through the sorter,
chickens, saws, the springs that close screen doors.
Sensual only in bed, and then of prodigious appetite,
the headboard slapping the wall
night after night,
tap tap tap tap.

The burden of the understood,
the knowledge assumed,
the meaningful glance,
the wrench to be fetched at once
but never defined or described,
the inarticulate shrug and guffaw.

Once a year he'd sit on the kitchen linoleum
to carve Jack o' lanterns with us.
Half an hour, once a year.

Deeds were Dad's speech:
his sixteen hours of sweat a day,
his neck eroded into arroyos by weather,
his shoes like Leninist bronzes of shoes,
his shins knobby from cows' kicks,
the trim body he weighed every morning,
the handsome hands tough as the emery wheel
that honed axes and scythes,
the sound of that wheel,
and the hard water dripping onto it
from a rusty can.
A workman and his tools—
a diligent cathedral mason.

All is gone now like snow water under culverts,
gone in flames like the space left when a board is sawn,
the gap where metal has been sundered.

And a little water flows,
a few apple twigs broken by blizzards drift past,
a trickle of water hard with minerals.
I still feel you were killed
by the stupid doctors,
taking bone marrow samples
and ignoring your quiet, "There's something there,"
taking twelve long weeks to wear away your mettle.

Anger washes away, quietly, beneath the road,
in dented pasture culverts;
loam scours the corrugations with obsidian tears.
A whole year has flown
since you disappeared.
I see again from this great distance
the husbanded manure spread on the fields,
feel again the icy furrows soften underfoot like melting lead

Father, you are coming back under a different name:
Memory.

My Muse

My muse grunts below ground,
pressing two hundred pounds.

My muse knots a new string on his yo-yo,
walks the dog on the kitchen lino.

In today's rushes, my muse slouches
with Brando on tenement couches.

My muse goes each week to work
while I stay home and creatively shirk.

My muse has hair on his feet
and keeps an iambic beat.

My muse kisses my lips
after rejection slips.

My muse likes hot wine, hot cha, hot milk—
and metaphors slick as silk.

My muse says I'm not working at peak;
he *is*, he says, giving both biceps a tweak.

Fur-Face

Fur-face in a night cap
was good for the rap.
True!
The story *had* to be true.
Great Grammy was long gone.
There wasn't so much as a chipped amethyst brooch
or a scuffed high-buttoned shoe
of her left.
Little Red chewed her lip, forlorn, aghast, bereft.
Tick, tock, said the grandfather clock.

In better days, dear G. G. would step
from her ground floor bedroom—
Bible read, grey net over grey hair;
all set to get on with the day,
primed for giggling and play.
An hour of songs, rhymes and tickles;
of counting fingers and toes.
Now she schlepped a bright felt board.
Now she knitted winter socks.
Tick, tick, said the grandfather clock.
Next she peeled a ripe Baldwin.
Then, adept, she folded a napkin
into a swan or a pickle.
She spun muffins of fun from thin air.

Each new letter or word was a comet,
each tale a delicious surprise.
She played all the parts
from upstarts to mules to eggheaded fools.
Her intention, she said, was "Voice Lessons."

But, as aforementioned, Great Gram had proved fickle.
She couldn't be found upstairs or down.
Further, the house held only one bath.
So come that daily midnight dreary,
bladder weary, Little Red faced the wrath of the pack.
Night Terrors:
The wallpaper's swags of philodendron,
rosettes of begonia,
convulsed into galloping bodies
and regiments of keen teeth.

Deep dens emptied out,
spilling a fearsome rout.
On either hand a
a milling band of snarling beasts,
seeking feasts.
Prowling, howling, pushing;
loping, re-grouping, overlapping, jaws snapping,
grim predators swarmed like warm oil
along both walls.
Each fur face flourished a tail-flag
like a Roman guidon.
Much to fear:
the pack's all here.

That hall was dreadful— dark, endless;
and Little Red was friendless.
Unwilling to be a wolf's diet,
she tried to tiptoe, to step quiet-
ly over the floor cold as glass.
Her tongue turned to hash-meat.
Sinister wraiths, leaping, creeping,
slinking, stinking in the gloom;
muzzles bloody, paws muddy
(paws bigger than a Woodsman's hand),
intent on reaping sweet girl flesh,
the wolves wove a howling mesh of doom.

Swifter than the charging bear
or fleeing hare,
the vulpine herd moved ahead, intent
as armored legions;
faster and faster,
without disturbing a hair of lath or plaster.

On the return gauntlet to bed,
the dread hall seemed a little shorter;
nevertheless, the slavering wolves
still milled, ready to kill.
Frightened Little Red ran in fear
year after year.
Tick, tock.
Poor dear!

Gross Anatomy 101

Always right, you schemed
to be right after death.
And so for eight months
why incisions
have been your secret delight,
giving answers to questions
about deafness, joint replacements,
pregnancies,
breast cancers.

One of a select ten thousand
without breath,
you spin: the center of a universe
of intensity and knives.
Soon you are preserved in bowls, in sterile jars,
in slides, in scribbled notes,
in student brains that ponder you
from cranial sutures to hammer toes.

Your cutting jibes
echo in the windowless hall.
Your breathless laugh has tuck-pointed
the damp stone walls with glitter.
And so for eight months
why incisions
have been your secret delight,
giving answers to questions
about deafness, joint replacements,
pregnancies,
breast cancers.

Then comes the fire,
the padded envelope—
and home.

One Nest, One Burrow

The autumn orchard spreads its jewels
before us fork-ed fools.

One nest, one burrow
close to alfalfa's furrow:

the oriole's woven pouch,
the ground hog's flinty couch.

One yearns to weep, one grieves to cheer
at this pair of masterpieces waiting there.

Heavenly avatars of awe
lie hidden at their cores.

They crave
to be appraised.

O to be a gemologist
wielding a loupe on a lariat.

I, poet, desire encyclopedias
like the grand *Britannica*

on a Jeffersonian stand or table.
I dearly wish to be able

to describe Nature's miracles
in stanzas lyrical.

Every sense ablaze
I crave

to mine each small fact
splendidly packed

into this pastoral scene.
I lick clean

the dewy plate of desire
which reflects blinding sunrise fire.

The pocket-nest:
a sight to be blessed.

Wisps of Grandma's gray hair
feature prominently there.

Threads from a denim sleeve
wrap roulades of apple leaves.

Grain bag string,
a flap of a dead robin's wing.

Straw is crocheted in purls,
in bangs, in curls.

Strands of raveled wool
seem to braid in the morning cool.

You realize it's darning,
it's tapestry; you're fawning

at the contrapuntal sights
of scheduled architectural flight.

As to the hole: it's a trip
to perch on this unpretentious lip.

Concerning that solitary "hog,"
this beast logs

few hours in the deadly light of day;
he hides away

pressing cider
in his larder.

He loves fruit.
From his shadowy lair he scoots.

Shy guy, Hog flirts
with shadow's fluttering skirts.

The Odyssean discoverer's helm
is charmed and overwhelmed

by the pleasure
of this treasure.

Pretensions fly away
confronting infinitely complex display.

O God above,
if You love
me, I need to prod
You to send me more: more serene,
more truly miraculous scenes.

The Civil War Ink Bottle

"'A course I like to think it's real.
A thing like this, wordless on a windowsill—
sky blue glass, hobnailed, with original cork—
makes you think; even, if you'll excuse my sayin', *dream*.
It's a pure pleasure to turn a thing like this-here
in your hand; turn it 'round, around.

"I like to think it's real—real, genu-wine.
It's a magic carpet that carries you
to a burning swamp, or on your belly
in the jelly of mud behind a boulder on a
mountain slope, pebbles and stray rocks tumbling,
dry brush crackling below,
Minie bullets whizzing round like mad bats—
or baby birds just hatched, can't find their way.

"You know, Grant could have thrown this-here at
a Contraband—or a horseman bringing bad news.
Lee could have sketched a quick drawing –a map
of a boot-brown river he remembered
from the July before.
Don't matter what side. You smell the rank sweat,
horse manure, burned beans, latrines and the smoke—
the G. D. smoke. Shoot!
Some volunteer like that New Yawk poet-coot
perched on a rickety milking stool could have dipped here,
penning a page to the worried Mam of a blind son.

"Museums have their place, sure do. But I
prefer to hold history in my hand, look it in the eye.
(Hand me that stick of kindling.)
Well, anyhow, it's not just the rippled glass.
Take a gander at
the cork stopper with initials R. U.?
Now that's a curiosity, I swan.
Should have been lost early on: R. U., R. U.—
as if asking a question of the past.

"This bottle could have travelled like Tom Thumb:
in a horse's ear, in a cow's triple gut.
North and South and then West, and West again—
endless marches with blistered feet.
'Minds me of a book from the li'berry,
'bout Andersonville and the Dead Line.
A hell of skeletons ragged to their knees, a gawd awful stench,
that miraculous spring on the hill—
and a low, incessant moaning ...'

"Misssus thinks I'm just an old silly
to sit here in Grandsire's maple rocker
and flit worthless war tales 'cross my skull.
She reckons I choose a time of day
when the light comes in that winder;
it sets the 'hull bottle all-agleam. Yes;
I set the rocker right across the beam.

"Imagination doesn't hurt a soul.
I see the bottle swaddled in a mite of quilt
like a fussy young'un, see it in the heel of a grey sock.
I see it gleamin' on a bleedin' birch stump
next a skillet of bacon grease and moldy tack.

"How it catches your eye,
a coiled copperhead sleek with oil? Don't it now, don't it?
Gee-hoss-a-fat, man, how I do go on!
All this loafing and gabbing. There's plenty
chores to do! Wire to walk!
Honest to God! Daylight's a' wastin'!"

In the Horse

"Shaved from head to toe,
ritually bathed in spring water,
under cover of darkness and dunes
we climb the padded rope
to the small hatch
cupped in the exaggerated rose
of the stallion's genitals.

"We dozen are the best left
after ten years from home.
Each carries two corked stirrup jugs
(one new wine, one water).
We have skins of jerky and hard cheese;
we have covered pails for waste.
Mute, we perch in rows of shallow rifts
cut into the thick pine sides
of this impressive stud, this awesome beast—
bigger than a Friesian plow horse,
bigger than a giant oak.
Tongue flicking, dry mouth agape—
a wounded viper seeking shade—
Time crawls.

"Two hundred sticky air holes concealed
among the heroic waves of mane
prove insufficient.
Faint sea breezes coax them to play tunes
like those from Pan's flute.
Odysseus fans himself
with his fav felt hat.
Neoptolemus giggles,
squeals like a cornered rat.
(He's our youngest.)

"We breathe lightly.
No banter.
Trying to get comfortable,
we wrap up in sweat-stained linen cloaks.
We nap.
Time crawls; crawls, hisses and spits
like a hovering siren.
Will the wary Trojans accept this 'gift,'
breach the impenetrable walls
to let it canter in, brimming with cold steel?

"Sun finally floats above the green-black hills.
Now the weird flute grows dim, but
the lookouts on the walls raise an alarm.
Sea-dark Others slither past in slime.
Women keen—we know not why.

"Soon we overhear slaves instructed,
hear cut stones shifting in their ancient beds.
Then from the general din
comes the unmistakable cricket chorus
of bronze chisels
removing lips of old mortar.
We nod heads at one another
in the increasingly humid dark.
We sip, stretch.
Time begins to run.

Fine Shining Weather: Three Poems for John Muir

I

Muir at Bottom

This was my "method of study." I drifted about from rock
To rock, from stream to steam . . . I asked the boulders
I met whence they came and whither they were going.

Except the Sabbath, New Year's, the Fourth,
they worked every day,
clearing 80 acres in Marquette County.
Fountain Lake Farm they called it—
oak and hickory and a small glacial lake cirqued in lilies.
"Old Man Muir works his kin like cattle,"
the neighbors said.

After eight years of clearing, fencing, plowing,
the land worn out by wheat and corn,
they moved to a virgin half section six miles southeast:
Hickory Hill.

There was no water at Hickory,
so John (the oldest boy) was put to digging the well.
Ten feet down he struck hard sandstone.
Driven by his own competitiveness
and his fanatic Pa,
he chopped away week after week.
Lowered in a bucket, he hammered
and chiseled lower.
At eighty feet was overcome by
"chokedamp" (carbon dioxide).
Lowered the next day
he put spiders and flies that crept near
out of harm's way.

He had chopped acres above ground;
now he grubbed away below—
His first solitary excursion into nature.
At 6 each morning his clockwork early-rising machine
tipped him from stiff quilts.
He tugged on frozen boots and socks,
descended to rocky pastures.
As he chipped away, he invented gadgets to whittle:
Pyrometers, waterwheels, automatic horse feeders—
things to save work at Hickory Hill.
they kept him going,
these "dear, airy nothings
in the most confused corner of his heart."
He scored rock, scored rock,
at ninety feet, hit water.

Always after that had a throat irritation,
began to tip out at one,
so as to have five hours to read.

The contact with rock did its work.
Months of intimacy at bottom
made him an observer,
so that when he ascended Yosemite
(Uzumaiti, "The Grizzly," of the Ahwahneechees),
he alone saw tiny evidence of rock polishing—
and knew what he saw.

He alone hiked back far enough
(Scots mountain goat flying a pennant of auburn beard),
following tiny streams of fine gray silt.
In a confused corner of the Upper Merced,
he found old ice.

II

A Leaf, A Drop, A Crystal

—May 1871, Emerson journeys to Yosemite to meet Muir.

Morning at the sawmill, dewy pine resin tweaking my beard.
suddenly as I bent over a slab,
I saw long legs on a piebald mustang.

It was he, my shepherd!
He is 68, the star of his own wagon,
but he came from San Francisco to see *me*,
John O'Mountain,
with sawdust in my hair.

I shook his white hand with my calloused, pitchy paw.
I could have lain the log I was slabbing at his feet.
I could have lain at his feet myself.

And so began an adventure never imagined.
His conversation shook me as if I had climbed a hundred-foot fir
set rocking in the heart of a Sierra gale,
close to lightning and Aeolian music.
There is nothing like a storm;
there is nothing like wild, hurtling talk
that saws close to the heartwood of life.

It was a wonder to show him the meadow, the dome,
how it cascades down like molten silver, frozen in granite.
I offered him what little I had: my poor sketches,
my pressed mariposas,
my best trillium, incense cedar, canyon oak.
I was charged in his presence as when I rode the avalanche.
I was Elijah in his chariot of fire.
I have been days in the presence of an angel,
shared corned beef and tea.
My whole body was ear,
hanging on his words.
They covered me as moss covers cold quartz.

He, too, walked out in storms
And felt the emotions in the waving boughs.
He knows nature's lesson:
That the clearest way into the universe is through a forest.

I told him my fondest dream:
How this wild cathedral must be a park, a new thing entire.
I told how Catlin envisioned it first, back in '32.
"A nation's park, containing man and beast,
in all the wild freshness of their nature's beauty."
That's how Catlin put it.

An artist, he could see it all—Indians, buffalo and prairie.
Preserved.
All one being.
But his idea was revolutionary, ahead of its time,
and nothing could save the Mother of the Calaveras Grove.
They peeled her bark and sent it to London,
as Pocahontas was packed off with John Smith.

Now we have forty square miles, a state preserve,
thanks to Mr. Lincoln.
But it is not enough.

I told him the Ahwahneechee word for big tree, "Wawona."
He told me of Thoreau's last words:
"Moose, Indian."
Time runs out.
I remember when I first set eyes on Nature,
there on Mendota's bonny banks.
I read, "In the woods is perpetual youth."
I rubbed my eyes, glad I could see.
I decided then to shoulder my plant press, leave Madison's lecture halls,
walk again into wilderness.
I found I could scale cliffs as a spider ascends a hollyhock.
All the world was below me,
and every day a holiday.

That was yesterday.
Today we rode to the grove, thirteen horses in all.
I would ordinarily walk, a crust of sourdough in my pocket.
One hears and sees more, walking.
But for his sake I rode.
Oh, what a day. I am weary.
I stuff my mouth with bitter herbs and write on.

I wanted him to stay in my great bedroom of the night,
to sleep under the stars of my Sierra temple.
But he is frail,
and his friends urged him away, to Clarke's Inn.
I said, "You are yourself a Sequoia.
Stop and get acquainted with your big brethren."
But they would not let him.

I would willingly walk to Concord to hear him again.
He says he is making a List of Men—
and I shall be on it.

III

There Was This Power ... (John Muir, 1838-1914)

—Battling the "money changers and the water changers."

There was this power in his voice.
Sometimes it seemed to come
from the muscles in his back
(farmboy's muscles).
Sometimes it came from his throat
(where the loon nested);
from the whirling air above his unkempt head—
even from the cold front straddling the vast horizon.

He wanted to use it, this power—
not to move mountains
but to preserve them, leave them as He made them.

Resting under hemlock, resting under pine,
his power renewed itself at earth's green breasts,
at her blue thighs
where bottomless crevasses echoed
with shale displaced by his boot,
where he sheltered behind glacial erratics
to chew his healthy crumbs.

As far from the "hoofed locusts" of Yosemite
as he could go, he went;
as far from the "mechanical beetles"
who, he said,
should not be allowed to "mingle their gasbreath
with the breath of the pines and waterfalls."
He wanted "the money changers and the water changers"
out of his temple.

He wanted his voice
To save the wilderness for unborn generations.
He said, "Damn Hetch-Hetchy!
As well as dam for water-tanks our cathedrals."
He said,
"to let sheep trample so divine a place
is barbarous."

Called "a tramp" by his foes,
he said,
"Don't pity me, pity yourselves.
You stay at home, dry and defrauded of all the glory I have seen.
Our souls starve in the middle of abundance."
He sauntered across her grassy bosom,
across "The Range of Light,"
taking notes, keeping them under his belt.

After camping with T. R. in Yosemite in aught-three,
he said,
"I was surprised to find
he knew so much of natural history."
That hyperactive "pure act" and Muir
(in a canary yellow short-pants outfit bought for the occasion),
"got lost" and slept in a sequoia grove,
resting among the cinnamon pillars,
the fragrant capitals.

Both liked a hard ride, a hard walk,
They were equals in one other thing:
Both excelled at talking without listening.
Roosevelt called the grove "a vaster and more beautiful cathedral
than was ever conceived by any human architect."
Muir said
"I never before
had so interesting, hearty and manly a companion.
I fairly fell in love with him."

Yosemite seemed safe for a while,
until some city got thirsty,
and Muir had to gird his power about him again.

In aught-nine, Taft would not camp out,
but he listened well.
Muir persevered against "ravaging commercialism,"
"the Almighty Dollar."
Eventually the long fight for Hetch-Hetchy
wore him down.
"It's killing me," he said,
missing Louie.

Pneumonia squeezed him in its vise,
and he died,
tipped out of life.
The "camping tramping tree-climbing scrambler ...
the rank, cantankerous, and withal lovable Scot"
was silent.

It was just as well.
He never had to see those muddy reservoir banks where nothing grew.

Iris Is Last

For Shem Pete (1896 - 1989), whom USA Today *called "the last of his people," and for the Denaina Athabascans of Cook Inlet, Alaska*

After silence, music.
After the soft blue,
the hard pod.
Iris is the rattle
as they remember Shem.
Iris is last.

Before the Denaina carved homes for pebbles,
there was the sturdy stalk, the musical wand.
Before they strung kindling with puffin beaks,
there were the twirling aspen leaves.
Before they heard the carved raven chatter,
there was frail iris nattering in the Knik wind.
Iris is last.

When the people walked the flats digging *k'tilla*,
their shins rustled dry iris pods.
Children jousted with them—
chanting, humming.
Iris is the rattle.

After silence, music.
After morning, evening.
We remember him in the evening
when fire casts riddles on walls.
Iris is the riddle
as they remember him,
the singer whose name means "sing."

Before white man flocked thick as cotton grass,
thick as reeds where terns nest,
there was iris blue as song.
Shem Pete steps slow on beaded soles.
Iris is the rattle.
Dancers he taught move in his honor.
Stories he told fall from their lips
as they remember him in the evening.
Iris is the rattle
as they remember him.

When the wind shakes the rattle, when that rattle starts,
the song sings itself.
Shem's song sings itself—
the papery rattle, the sturdy stalk.
Iris is the rattle
as we remember him.
Iris is last.

The Translator's Grandson

It's almost too warm
in the Translator's house,
buffeted by July Fourth wind from the Bering.
My host, a tall, soft-spoken gentleman,
crosses the plywood floor without making a sound.
His singular occupation is translating
from English into Siberian Yupik.
For five years
he has been working
with a swarm of White missionaries
to translate that tusk of Civilization,
The New Testament.

A reporter flown in from Anchorage,
I ask, "What is the hardest word
you have had to translate?"
Not hesitating an instant,
he says, "Grace.
Grace."

Meanwhile his grandson
jumps up and down on the couch—
a tiny, seal-eyed kangaroo,
watching television.
(The volume's turned way down.)
Assuming I need help,
the toddler points at the black and white screen.
"Dog," he says.
"Dog."

Learning Eskimo Dancing/ Lighting Up the World

The night is falling.
It is evening and it is dark.
But when the moon comes out,
The brightness—
It lights up the world.
—Yupik elder William Tyson of St. Marys

Eskimo dancing is for happiness.
—Paul Tiulana, founder of the King Island Dancers

For Max, who afforded me entrée.
And for Inez, who made me welcome.

Duck Hunt, Skidoo, Prayer Song—
Now we are learning Eskimo dancing.
It is the way of St. Mary, the way of William Tyson.
Tyson puffs if he climbs the steps to the practice room,
but he avoids the elevator.
"I eat too much," he says, rubbing his stomach,
after puffing up the sixteen steps.
The life of tradition can reflect the longevity of lungs and stomach.

The group is children and their moms,
a few single women.
Each struggles along at his own pace.
No one is ever pushed.
There is encouragement, demonstration—
but not remonstration.
This is the correct way.

But when Tyson settles into drumming, he may play tyrant.
You never know how many choruses he'll insist on,
even in public performances at the Museum,
continuing until he catches that glimmer of correctness,
of intensity, of commitment.
He hammers his drum like an anvil,
commanding all, immersion.

In the Chup'ik tradition, men kneel
and women stand behind as they dance.
Yupiks beat their skin drums from above,
Inupiats beat from beneath the translucent gut drumhead.
(Sometimes the gut is airplane fabric, now, of course.)

Yupik men dance with hand fans
of driftwood and feathers.
William and his wife Marie fashion fans with dyed goose feathers.

Wild feathers are outlawed now, protected.
(There ensues a pause in practice to allow
an ironic discussion of how the Real People
cannot gather feathers even from birds dead on the beach.)

Women dance with fans fringed with waving caribou beard.
The fans are woven grass, finger loops woven on.
Feathers and hair draw the eyes, waving,
outlining arm motions like light drawn on air.

Everyone wears gloves—
some beaded hide, some ordinary white Sunday gloves.
"My hands feel naked if I dance without gloves,"
comments drummer Ben Snowball.
"With gloves, I'm more in the mood—
it just feels good."

The drumbeat is a brook rippling over shale,
soothing as Gregorian
No matter how it thrums the ceiling,
it is not noise like rock 'n roll.
It is noise like Niagara, Victoria.
Ears never ring afterward.

Welcome Song,
Bookworm,
Skidoo.

"What's this motion?" Rose asks
When Tyson flaps his feathered hoops in new choreography.
"I just made it up," says thee wily stickler for tradition,
poker-faced, swigging Sunkist Orange ® from a can.
His throat is always dry.
He puffs up the 16 steps.

Besides the new moves,
there is new dance about
"Traveling along and having a good time going somewhere,"
Tyson demonstrates.
"This is steering the car," he says,
arms extended in front, gripping an imaginary wheel.
"But then we have to stop for a red light,
folding at the elbow.
"The train is hollering!"
he explains with comic recoils of alarm.
"The train is hollering at me,
so I got scared."
He chuckles at his own vaudeville.

Seal Hunt:
Rowing out onto the ocean in kayaks.
Looking for seals (hand shading the eyes).
Spotting prey.
Rowing closer.
Hurling harpoons.
Rowing fast and desperate, toward the carcass
before it sinks from sight.
Pulling in the seal.
"Tow it from back here, like this,"
Tyson says, miming weight at the end of his invisible line.

Prayer Song,
Duck Hunt,
Welcome Song,
Bookworm.
Igloo: Yung, a yung a high; yung a yung a high.
Yo ho ho, yo ho ho.
The snow must drift firmly for cutting blocks.

Eskimo Ice Cream:
Stirring it up, whipping the oil until it's really fluffy.
Placing the bowl on the floor.
Pulling parka over the head.
Picking up the bowl.
Walking toward the door, opening it.
Serving yummy ice cream to friends.
Swallowing deep and with satisfaction:
GULP, GULP, GULP.

"Don't get scared to move your body,"
Tyson instructs the troupe one week.
"Your body should be moving, not your head,"
he adds, meaning, "Don't think too much."
"I heard somebody fell asleep on his feet dancing the other day.
That's O.K."
"When I was young, I could dance all night,"
he adds as an aside.

This is the winter of the Gulf War,
and he has pinned a yellow bow to the breast pocket
of his red and blue plaid flannel shirt.

Prayer Song,
Nunivak,
Duck Hunt,
Igloo:
cutting out the blocks with an ivory snow knife.

The beat is a brook, a waterfall,
Victoria, Niagara,
Soothing as Gregorian.
You could listen for hours.

It is energizing, yet soothing, a muscular lullaby.
After all, Paul Tiulana says,
as the odorous squares of polar bear fur
are distributed to the elders
in celebration of a first polar bear kill,
"Eskimo dancing is for happiness."

Kissing the Frog

His entrance is announced by flies.
A raw wound on one shoulder weeps—
a pitchfork graze.
One shriveled hindfoot drags.
In his carbuncled, rheumy gaze there is spite
for all my species (once his).
for all my sex (that cursed him thus);
there is hatred and envy's alum.
There is only one key to his quandary—
my kiss, freely given.

My feet in thin silk are chill bottles from the cellar,
my tongue flicks among ashes.
My wooden hands creak into fists,
and pink nails stab greasy palms.

I bend:
The taste is of moss—
and misery,
of salted feathers, bile, gizzard grit.
His bloodless amber eye signals
a kiss on the cheek is insufficient.
I bend closer.

A Baby Walks

I

a baby
holds onto
the arm of a sofa

he is just ten months
just ten

he thoughtfully fingers
the nap of the upholstery

he looks to see
If anyone is watching

he lets go
he walks!

and this is the precise instant
when the Winds of Time
(which are undeniable
and also known as sirocco)

push back the waters
so the Chosen can escape;

a simoon from The One God
pushes back the ponderous waters
to reveal a path of soppy land

and the shape of the ancient waters
is like eggy dough
cut down through the middle
by floury hands;
and the tender halves part from each other
revealing the pastry board between,
beneath

and the baby
(suddenly overcome by his adventure
and perilous new exposure to carpet)
plops onto his butt

II

the baby laughs

oh, lordy, what now??

Places

Sitka

Buttercups, buttercups, buttercups.
Salmonberries, salmonberries, salmonberries.
Cedar, cedar, cedar.
Herculaneum, lupine, beach pea.
Dogwood, dogwood, dogwood.
Rain, rain, sun.

Bumper sticker:
"Don't blame me. I voted for Willie Nelson."
Bumper sticker:
"Tongass old growth, It's Wirth defending."
Bumper sticker:
"Hang onto our rain forest."
Rain, rain, sun.

Roots, rocks, crevices.
Waterfalls, mountains, mist.
Eagle, eagles, eagles.
The upward spiral of Swainson's thrush
piercing the underbrush with a spear of song.
Moss, moss, lichen.
Rain, rain, sun.

Cones, seeds, buds.
Fucus, alder, columbine.
False lily of the valley, blow down, wind.
Cedar, hemlock, cedar.
Shingle, driftwood, island.
Bark, grass, petroglyphs.
Shells, beads, arrows.
Limpets, canoes, herring roe on kelp.
Planks, oil, labrets.
Deer heart, beach pea, Devil's Club.
Salmon steamed in skunk cabbage.
Boxes, mats, blankets.
Rain, rain, sun.

Baranof, Veniaminov, Gajaa Heen.
Otter, incense, icons.
Fairweather Cove, Shot Gun Alley, Winchester.
Rhododendrons, lawns, roses.

Lincoln, Katlian, Sawmill.
Slip, seep, soak.
Dry, smoke, pickle.
Rain, rain, sun

Spears, totems telephone poles.
Baranof Motors, The Potlatch House, Ann's Tiques.
Row, cast, gaff.
Under rocks, gray crabs.
Overhead, gray clouds.
Gold mines, hatcheries, saw mills.
S.B. Daiquiri, *Blue Love*, *Tyee*.
Docks, rain, sun.

Sign:
"Don't even think of parking here."
Sign:
"Mad Jack's Wax Museum."
Sign:
"Uppity Women Unite."
Cedar, cedar, hemlock.
Kerf, knot, plait.
Rain, rain, sun.

Buttercups, buttercups, buttercups.
Cedar, hemlock, cedar.
Silver, soapstone, beads.
Slugs, puddles, tides.
A root puts its arm around the shoulder of a stump.
The upward spiral of Swainson's thrush
pierces the underbrush with a spear of song.
Indian River, Sealing Cove, Kiksadi Club.
Raven, raven, raven.
Raven, raven, raven
muscling head back in noisy protest.
Caw, caw, caw,
caw.

Cogs Within Cogs

Smoke on the water where the glacier drips.
Droplets on the yearling bear's fur.
The gleam in his eye signs, "What, are you nuts?"
when you try to shoo him off.

Vistas of trees disappear,
reappear like soldiers marching in a mist.
A mirage of hills like camels' humps
trots along the far shore of Berner's Bay.
Water percolates,
blurring the line
between earth and heaven.
Ravens gargle in spruce tops,
each bird polished by water
until it is an argillite totem.

Glinting, rushing, trickling,
water never stands still here.
It comes and goes like a turbaned genie
in elemental intercourses.
The exhalation of whales
condenses in puddles beneath entwined brambles.
Deer's breath falls into the ruts of deer hoofprints,
steams from a mug of Earl Gray tea.
The heel of wind's palm irons flat the waves.

Like cogs, dolphins turn thru the sea—
as if circling instead of arcing.
Each sleek back echoes another, cog after cog revolves
in water's lush clockwork.
Mists sidle skyward through Devil's Club and skunk cabbage:
tulle streamers, feeling their way along avalanche chutes
like fingers in white cotton gloves,
reading the mountains' Braille.
Probing upward, they flow,
liquid strokes penned on endless scrolls.

Hemlocks a hundred feet tall sway in the wind.
Lichens, two-leafed pines, heath worts, huckleberries,
and prickly panax have no umbrellas.
The shape of wind on water glints everywhere,
even in brief dents left by the feet of water striders.
In the shallows, salmon flit from salmon shape
to salmon shape: currant-striped paper-dolls.

Bays, cascades, waterfalls:
Waves, billows breaking up rills and riffles,
submerged moraine singing.
Luscious foam dashes beaches and bays.
Empty shells woggle as the tide turns.
Fallen logs swell, are felted and furred
with half a foot of moss (mostly yellow).
Somehow it all adds up to a spell,
a salty aura that embraces, reassures.

Hail is our Grail.
Water beads moss
and carves rock,
micron by micron.
Floods sluice arroyos
more delicate than circuit boards.
Nothing as direct as open roses.

Water drips, drips, slips from shaggy hemlocks,
enamels orange salmon berries
as they swell drupe upon drupe, cog upon cog.
Mist to drop,
drop to mist.
Plop.
Repeat.

Drops, droplets, cups, eddies, swirls, ripples.
Millions of droplets forming, belling to their ultimate expansion
and then falling, falling—
onto something wet, soggy.

Here,
one *can* step into the same river twice—
rain forest by name.
During downpours, wet black scallops
slip in an endless conga line down Hermit Street—
like LP's morphing into floppy discs.
Wet, oh bless'ed wet.

It Pushes

(Ivoo, Barrow/Utqquiavik; 600 years BPE)

"This world is but canvas to our imaginations."
—Henry David Thoreau

It pushes.
A mouse shriek curls from Auntie
squatting in the entrance tunnel,
roasting flippers.
Grandma's best oil lamp shudders,
rises in the smoky air
like a breaching bow-head;
then falls, casting burning moss wicks
onto the baby.
Startled, he thrusts his arms up, up
toward the ceiling;
his mouth forming a silent wet O.

Slick as a seal,
the near-shore ice
slides onto the beach
like a walrus mounting his mate,
like a husband's sweaty thigh over mine.
It pushes.

Shock's silence begins.
Nothing to see
but tumbled chunks of salty jewels,
groaning, changing shape—
consolidating on the trembling, fractured shore.

It pushed.
Big Sister screamed,
then screamed again, a smothered cry
somewhere under the shifting tumble.
Wails, wails on every side.

Under Mendenhall

"In every walk with nature, one receives far more than he seeks."
—John Muir

An icy Cornell Box of the past
stutters toward a tropical future.
Teased by terror,
we spelunk around a giant's ear lobe—
insatiable for the inscrutable
within the unstable.
Here are the snows of yesteryear—
Liquefied; tickling, coating the congealing tongue.

With each cautious step forward
even the possibility of warmth
recedes.
Ordinary gravel underfoot,
but enclosed in a seashell's narrowing spiral—
gemmy blue, foxglove glue, bruise blue and dripping.
Glistening crystal on all sides,
shoulders on steroids seem to shrug;
elbows, heels, buttocks—all stacked wetly,
giving us the fisheye.
Angles convert to curves with every drip,
every hidden seep or fall.

Feet slip,
eyes sip
until a shiver warns.
Blue satin tuffets strike a pose;
clear burbling rivulets give off essence of Tongass.
A mammoth's digestive rumble
sends a tumble of uncut gems
over a sheer precipice.

Brash Ice

Auke Lake, Juneau

"I photographed all things,
All things as happening...."
—John Ashbery

Steps away, a moose melts into cover
like a sugar cube becoming one
with a white mug of hot milk.
On the far shore,
a timber-hauler shifts gears,
harvesting the Tongass.
Otherwise, silence; no one in sight.

Along this near shore,
the house of cards shuffles its frame:
translucent, glittering;
a flotilla of tinkling crystals
falling and rising with each
exhalation of icy wind
like a Big Game stadium "wave."
As our sky-blue kayaks change shape
(blue weather balloons),
blue ripples and reflections
skim over the open water,
encouraging endless galaxies of chandeliers
to join their hoarse voices
in a cold choir
only we can hear.

Brief gusts parade from shore to shore,
plunge like dragon flies, spying drones
or feeding gulls;
forming a nano-second cluster
of herring eggs.
Spicules break from the edge of the floe
to spell out in crystal twigs
some ancient runes.
Jaws, tongues, lips and paws
Chew pebbles, slap, sift glacial flour, lick,
caress the prow.

A rolling crackle of frost,
unfolding a paper of pins,
sugar shingle,
slosh and tinkle.
Gurgle.

A lace of froth trembles along the hull.
Chuckle, gurgle.

See and Release

In my travel article, I told of the quiet,
the low knolls covered with birch and black spruce,
the reed thickets,
the tea-colored water steeped in centuries of peat,
the quaking bog where we stepped from our canoe
only to wet our feet,
the black and turquoise striped dragon flies
and the water strider that came to lunch.

But I didn't tell about the 26-inch rainbow
in the channel between two lakes,
the lunker the color of peat,
all its pink and white spots khaki and old olive
from advanced age.
Husband and son didn't believe my story.
Then the rainbow, charmed, swam by again—
as if to confirm my tale.

Even though I had no urge to catch that trout,
I wanted to save it for myself.
I wanted to return another day
to glimpse him against the soft, floating bank.

In my travel article, I wrote about the mosquitoes,
the loons,
the two abandoned beaver dams,
how the Athabascans came here 9,000 years ago
when the ice sheet receded along the Susitna,
creeping backward like a cold car stalled in reverse.

In this poem, I write about the magic fish—
but not where to find him.
I can play at two games.
The fish plays at swimming and hiding.
I play at see and release.

Gold Creek, Ouzel

In truth,
this is not Gold Creek proper—
but a minor tributary,
trickling in from the East.
It forms a neat, mossy waterfall
of shallow green steps—
silently, almost reluctantly, falling
into the needled pleats
of the pine thicket
surrounding the ball field.

How can that dear dun birdling
take her short flights on the flinty stone
beneath the soft, flowing water—
viewed as through a wavy window pane?
How can that feather-weight sprite
feed so on microscopic prey, hunting and pecking,
keeping balance and breath
in the clear stream?

I have seen her here three times now.
She is like a flash of the sunburned calf
of an incautious goddess,
wading, stepping from dappled clearing
to dappled shade.

Words for Shadows

Set to original music and a soundscape by composer Philip Munger, which was created to play continuously to accompany a gallery show of bronzes of oiled seabirds, sea otters, and others killed by the Exxon Valdez *spill, 1989. The original is in four parts. This is part one.*

The Places of Animals
caves of watery light
pearly grottoes
hollows
shallows
the flutes of shells
caves
grottoes
hollows
pristine shallows
cathedrals of waving kelp where the sun spreads like honey
fragrant spruce boughs
clean beach sand
gleaming ripples
spawning silvers and kings
caves, hollows
pristine shallows where yellow-legs dart
cohos
cathedrals of kelp where honey ripples
the flutes of shells
slick feathers
sleek fur

surfing seals
Breaker, breaker.
No matter where you went it was black.
The pearls that were their eyes.
There's a feeling of insult when a bird comes in just sopping with oil.
A feeling of insult.
No question about it.
It was so gross.

No matter where you went it was black.
We cried a lot.
People would come up and say,
"We just can't catch any more birds,"
and break out sobbing, sobbing.
It's beyond imagination.
The pearls that were.
I have wounds all over my hands from loons.
Once, I set a tape cassette on a rock, and the rock began to crawl away.
It was a seabird caked with oil.
A cormorant broke a hole in its breast trying to get clean.
It's beyond imagination.
Slippery, dead.
It was so gross.
We cried a lot.
The red eyes of loons.
We have to deal with birds, so we've got these tree huggers taking care of them.

$89,000 to save one sea otter.
What's an animal's life worth?
The rock began to crawl away.
It was so gross.
A cormorant holed her breast (single hull).
Deer curled up.
The only way we could identify a lot of the birds was by their beaks.
Single hull.
$89,000 to save one otter.
We have to deal with birds, so we've got these tree huggers.
No one wants to unseat the goose laying the golden egg that's oil.
I have wounds all over my hands from loons.
By their beaks you shall know them.
By the wounds.
By the stench.
Washing rocks, one by one.
What's an animal's life worth?

Circle of Stones

Mules and hens settle.
Too dark now for chores,
so everyone drifts to his circle of stones,
where his nerveless sitting raises puffs of ash.
Even Anansi the spider pauses in her weaving.
Leaves spiral down,
but the oaks will hold tight their crop
until The Big Times—
when top-hatted goblin hands out coppers
in the quarter.

Most ever thin goes in Car'lina firelight:
Brer Fox capers in riding boots that gleam
with reflected firelight.
Miz Possum shucks roasting ears,
passing them over her left shoulder
to her young'uns.
Ghosts and buried gold,
good harvests and ham gravy—
any story, no matter how far-fetched.
Anything goes under the languid fingers of Spanish moss.

A pail of cool water circles,
drinking gourd tied to the bail.
Sissy hands out cold corn cakes
smeared with the grace of grease.
The oldest hand hears lions
threading the cane next the Missisip'.
Bare toes sift cooled ash into red dirt.
In the dark, urgency dissolves,
tired backs relax.
Melancholy slips into the shadows
like a cat homing in on a mouse.
Anything goes around this token hearth—
any tale to hold off another morning.

Near Greenwood (Tulsa), 1821)

"This Royal? McNamara here.
Glad I caught you up, Son.
Thot Carl Sr. was gonna . . .
But never mind.

"Big do-ins on tap, lemme tell 'ya.
You mean to tell me you never did
no nigger knockin'?
Where you been, all your life?
It's jest one of the best, after dark.
(Get the darkies after dark, unnerstan?)
Steal a board, 20 feet, mebbe 22.
A 2x6. You got it. Gotta be solid.
Perch that sucker straddlin' the rolled-down
back windows. Right you are:
need a four-door for *this* blue rabbit hunt.
Next set two burly fellas back there,
holdin' it steady.

"Gas up. Mud the plates.
Then—no lights—
drive quiet on 'em, them walking 'a course,
Shove the board out the winder, and ka pow!
You can smell them bitches before you see 'em.
Last week we decked one chile
no higher than a fox hound's asshole.
Looked like a bunch 'o rags 'side the road.
That flesh makes a real nice sound
when it hits. Juicy, kind of.
Like throwing a cantaloupe onto macadam.
I think it's the head bone—
it's the dang ball findin' the glove pocket.

"Did ya know Buck and Everett go knockin' all the time?
Yep, them; an' Jeff Budbill, Tom Lennox
and that crazy cousin of his, Butch Spenser,
specially in winter when the moon's clouded.
Flatten them darkies after dark!
(I'm a poet and don't know it.)

"I'm tellin' ya, it's big doins for sure.
Hoods? Nah. Po-lees? They'll be helpin.
This is the big one, son.
The boys doin' it up right:
guns, yeah. Axes. Some guys 'll light torches.
Light 'em up, light 'em up!

"That they call "Black Wall Street" 'll burn
like ole MacDonald's pole barn—
all that crisp July hay, clouds of ash—black ash, oily,
stinking like a pig sty.

"Gonna be a big show; you gotta come.
If you're not, can I borrow your gun?
Solly's Tavern says they'll draw a free pint
for every bleedin' ear.
Gilyard? Clarence? I believe so.
But not Althea this 'a time.

Maybe postcards?
Where'll we dump all this shit?
Well, I think one a' them coal mines.
Dark to dark, ya' know.

The Effect of Recorded Hymns on Whitetails

Every afternoon at three
the carillon pipes up,
automatically sending "Blest Be the Tie that Binds,"
"Lord, When We Bend Before Thy Throne"—
you name it—
over gentle hills, through woods and hollers for miles around.

There's plenty of ethereal fodder in the 660 hymns
anointing the library of the Lutheran Synodical Conference.
Every afternoon "A Mighty Fortress is Our God,"
"Zion Stands by Hills Surrounded" or some such
barrels over blooming soybean rows
and congregations of corn,
gliding over swelling melons as easily as water
in Jacob Fork mopes over trashed radials.

Every afternoon at three
the whitetails fail to hearken to
"This is the Day the Lord Hath Made"—
or some hoary tune concerning flocks or grace,
sacrifice, sin or hope.
To bucks and does, the choir is so old hat that
hymns are no different from the thin crescendos
of passing cars and trucks,
a gentle, tinkling breeze slightly more musical than engine cough
but insufficient to halt their prayerful chewing.

Fireflies in Amish Country

Sunset's cool hands
lay on the day's blessing
as light settles down soft as feathers
behind the cornfield horizon
like a broody Leghorn in a hay mow.
The breeze is an asexual buss of clabber.

July in Pennsylvania.
Half an acre of lawn,
maintained by hand—
as perfect as a golf course
with no sand hazards.
After roast chicken,
carrots, stewed beans, applesauce,
we take our seats clustered on this expanse
to watch the fireflies muster.
The tiger cat makes the rounds,
soliciting pats.

Every one is relaxed
as a Jersey gently stripped.
No traffic, no leaf blowers;
no distant greeny glow of TV screens
or shrill of city cacophony.
Even the ubiquitous shiny pop-top
and the narrow glistening strip of cellophane
from a cigarette pack
are nowhere in view.

Here there is neither “chainsaw”
nor “carnival.”
Each verboten word
pierces the skin of belief
as a bullet bores through a ripe Spy.
Is “bioluminescence” allowed?
Does the dictionary end at “axle”
and “clawhammer,” at “clamp,”
at “footings” and “ridgepole”?
Is vocabulary tailored
like a farmer’s shirt collar?

We leave with a plastic bucket
of Pumpkin Snickerdoodles.
In our rearview mirror,
The hectic fireflies crisscross the lawn—
keep on keeping on,
delivering their coded verses.
Imagine each is an angel,
with skirts just long enough
to hobble her knees.

Borning Room

A low chamber one stoops to enter
built over a boulder elbowing through one wall—
a horse-size granite chunk cold-shouldering into the space,
a New England upwelling of obdurate ledge.

One steps up into this cramped chamber
from the main room with its wide fireplace.
No heat of its own but the flicker of pain, the gush of blood.
A damp cave, that dank grotto in the skull eyes turn to in prayer.

How many wives wore out on this rope bed
and joined their predecessors on the knoll
beyond the orchard?

The Final Approach

For John and Jim Ogonowski and their families

After the languid turn
into the final approach,
the North Tower's glass skin blinked once,
blinding him to everything but
the straight line of hay bales.
And he shuddered in REM sleep,
entering another September.

Ahead now was that blazing noon
of his youth—that great day
when his weight was sufficient
to hold down the tractor clutch.
As he lined up on the bales,
a frantic doe dashed for the stone wall.
Look here! Look here!

And John started to stand—
both to stop the tractor and
the better to see the nest.
As he rose, the box cutter at his nape
stuttered, plowing a thin red furrow.
And then under the blue sky
the roar of the engine
was drowned out by the human wails
of huddled, trembling leverets.

Buzzard Song

"Like lightning I stoop to conquer—
diving from cloud to ground,
waving at commuters at 20,000 feet.
Roadkill can fill me up.
Squirrel
Possum
Gulp
Swallow
House cat doesn't make you fat.
Maine coon in rigor
is good for the figure.
Ground pink pork chop
is my truck stop.
Indigestion
is out of the question.

"In Eden, I shared the serpent's tree.
A hiss or three,
and we drank deep by firefly's flitting lamp.
Lacking carrion,
I sipped barren nectar.
Then we escaped,
and menus improved.

"After a cutting kiss,
my beak drips blood
like a pirate's dirk.
In entrails no secrets—only succulence.

"No standing on ceremony
in my business.
I smell blood, I see gleaming wet blood pooling.
I dive right in,
then wipe my plate with fate.

"In my book, death is a treasure—
my reward for sitting watch.
Corruption is an anodyne."

The Hare in Tuckerman's Ravine

I

Thanksgiving. We camp in this monumental cirque.
(Thoreau saw it as a volcano's half-cone.)
We bed down in an uncomfortable nest of ancient cobbles.
The sky is a lace of cold, distant stars.
The moonlight has the shimmer of pewter.
The engravings of ice's infiltrations
all head in one direction:
Northwest to southeast,
northwest to southeast.

Midnight. Something rattles the cook pots.
It's a snowshoe hare,
leaving her habitat of blowdowns,
willows and conifer swamps
to seek a free lunch.

Lepus americanus.
Clocked at 27 mph.
It races with its massive hind feet
raised to its chest,
its small front feet digging in like Olympians' ski poles.

A squeak of frustration
as *lepus* leaps, then disappears
among infinite cobbles.

Life span: Three years possible.
Gestation period: 36 to 37 days.
Size of litter: Four the first year.

II

Summer. Fifty years later.
Without snow, the trail is
an endless, dry rapids.
Every alder seed underfoot
is expectant.
Each polished molecule of grit
tolls a hand bell in expectance.
"Moose. Indian."

If you visualize Thoreau with a raven
balanced like Poe's one-word bird
on his green coat's shoulder,
don't hang that naturalist halo too soon.

Henry David camped in Tuckerman's with friends.
One let the campfire get away,
consuming an ancient, dwarf forest.
On another outing,
cooking fish on a stump,
H.D. himself set afire a hundred acres near Walden.

The Snowshoe Food Web:
Wildflower to rabbit
to lynx
to eagle to bear.

Leverets suffer the hiccups
as they forage fir buds and wildflowers.

To complete digestion,
the Snowshoe must chew and swallow
certain of its turds.

Our hare has dog-paddled into history,
but we retain the *Appalachian Mountain Guide*:
A butter-yellow book
bent to the curve of a buttock.

Dig in.
Dig deeper.

First Words

Wolf's eyes are amber fires
low on the horizon, outside,
on the path up from water.

Cough.
The fires creep closer, two steps,
awaiting further instruction.

Cough, cough, sneeze.
Wolf looks expectant,
sits, his tail lifts briefly—
a willow leaf flipped into silhouette in a sunrise breeze.

Consonants chitter in the shadows.
Rock fall, out there,
where beasts belly forward
from the river bottom.
Soft thunder,
pebbles grinding, flaking into spear points,
a trickle of gravel into a footprint.

Cough, sneeze.
The fires wink.

Vowels shrill as insects
stream over the tongue
loose as rainwater,
then align in sudden phalanxes.
Beyond the circle of sleeping furs,
maggots churn in a dead bat's breast.

Cough. Dawn creeps in like fog lifting.
Parrot claws clenching and unclenching around a perch.

"Fish. Come,"
she says, holding out a moldy end
toward the cave mouth.
Wolf grins, comes, tame as a comma –
becoming Dog.

Willendorf, Early June

For my dear friend Teresa Ascone and her pocket goddesses

I

Midnight

Something wakes Da'vitt.
Slipping from his warm envelope of furs,
he tiptoes to cave mouth.
The Picket, the Sentry, is on guard,
as usual, but Da'vitt, the Carver,
is as cautious as the Ibex Hunter.
"Could be rock fall.
 Could be Trader or Outlaw,"
he muses.
South wind oozes the scent of rain.
After 10 minutes of listening hard –
and hearing nothing—
he nips back into his fur pocket.
(Dreams of lovers hover.)

II

Sunrise, Picket

Loud birds shout down Night.
Da'vitt is back in his dusty workshop.
His head swivels like an anxious owl's
to catch alarms,
as he runs his fingertips over bone blanks
cleaned of gristle:
heron, eagle, swan.
He chooses rabbit
and, with a curved blade,
his talented hands grave
a whistle.

Soon in strides Picket, breathing fast:
        "The wind has been shoving me
        right and left all night,"
        sez tall Keef'er,
        throwing back the hood of his cloak.
        "Good thing the Moon
        of Icicles on Hoods is past.
        I thought I heard nickering;
        but then I always think I hear nickering."
"You do a good job as Sentry, Keef'er,"
Dav'itt reassures his sleepy friend.
        "Mont'el was Picket last night;
the bloke's a hard nut.
I told him the tags of hair in his ears
were making him deaf.
Never could take a joke; only praise.
He's moons beyond his best running days,
but he still climbs crags like a bear
just out of hibernation."

III

The Son

Escaping the bother of toddler brother
(hearing Carver and Picket conversing),
Dav'itt's son, Too'un, saunters from the Creche,
peeling a roasted egg.
After gulping the toasted core,
he flicks the shell fragments to the floor.

"Were you raised in a thicket?"
The six-year-old carefully retrieves each speckled bit
and drops all into the small fire pit
of his Father's workshop.

In an aside to Keef'er, Dav'itt adds,
"I am teaching him the Kneel Down song."
On hearing that, Too'un begins softly singing:

Kneel down, bison.
Kneel down.
We have sharp arrows
with feathers red and yellow as yarrow.
Wait for the arrow.

We have long, long spears
good in all weathers.
Kneel down, bison.
Wait for the spear.

IV

The Drum

Too'un lingers. He longs for the Cave's drum
hanging high on a wall
among strings of dried crabapples.
"Where does the music go?" he asks.
"Music sings there, flows, sleeps there," Dav'itt replies,
jabbing a muscular finger into his son's rib cage.
"But it has wings.
In the darkest dark it sashays out
to dance with the wind."

"I want to grow up to be a drummer,"
Too'un says earnestly.
"Then you must pray, my son;
pray for such a blessing.
And be kind to the Drummer."

V

Lessons

"Listen closely, Son.
It is your morning to pick tinder.
'Remember the embers,' as you walk.
Take your net bag
and bring it back full of cones and bark.

"Look for hoof prints bigger than your heel.
Mark the location of nettles lower than your ankle.
If a stag antler is too heavy,
place it kneeling against a tree
so a Man may collect it.
(Remember the tree.)"

"Remember, too, the Hunter's Song:
    'The aurochs drinks.
    The reindeer drinks.
    Red deer, roe deer drink.'

"Remember: 'If you name the prey
it will stray.'

"And the Walking Song:
    'Open eyes; close feet.'"

VI

Venus and Carver

When Too'un's moccasins
can no longer be heard
skipping along the terrace,
Da'vitt slips the latest Venus down from her pegs.
He runs his fingertips
over her spiky tufts of hair;
smooth, tight plaits form a veil over her face,
concealing her expression.
Do her pale lips smile? Does she frown?
Only he knows.

After all, the graceful pattern
is close at hand.
Sleek as an otter,
the dream of beauty slides from the bubble idea
to his arthritic finger joints.
He drinks her in.
He hopes no one sees him kiss her.

The Lady has birthed in tens of shapes.
Da'vitt had seen samples at fall fairs:
a Woman spreading herself
with slick fingertips;
a Lady chiefly long, thin legs;
another with head small as an acorn.
One brandished an engraved horn.
Some were pierced for charms.
Strong arms are incidental to the design, he thinks.
But goddesses lacking
fruitful hips or buttocks
are missing the point.
On the other hand, no feet;
she must not flee.
No hands: she must not gather after the sixth moon.

"Some suggest I'm too adept
and mumble about 'a swelled head.'
Brave Hunters massaging their scars
by the night-fire, smirk.
'You can't roast art,' they grumble."

"I don't need plaudits or the thunder of validation.
I bend my gaze closer to my work
and let them sneer,
chewing their birch tar like bison
chewing cud.
These are not the bites of red ants.
These are green flies to wave away.
If I can snare it with my imagination, I carve it.
I peer into tomorrow.
I can carve sorrow."

Dav'itt caresses
Venus' milky breasts with his thumb.
He sneaks her another kiss.
He knows better than Little Miss Priss.
He reaches for his cache of red ochre.

VII

Too'un returns

Great Sun begins to station shadows.
Dav'itt, taking kissing strokes with
an arrow shaft smoother, can hear
Too'un running up the grand staircase,
inventing lyrics as he nears:

> 'This ibex drinks at the river.
> I have eleven arrows in my quiver.
>
> 'Oats and goats;
> smoke and oak;
> stone and bone;
> Wait for the spear. Wait for the arrow.

'Go eyes; stop feet.
Swallow the name of the prey.
Say prayers; greet Moon.
I have seven arrows....'

Dav'itt steps out on the wide, swept terrace to meet his son.
Impressionable Too'un bubbles over,
a spring freshet, a sea tide of news:
of "four feet clinking over moraine,"
of "the loop-de-loops of purple-green fliers."

VIII

Afternoon

Shaft smoother sands arrows.
Rock mortars grind einkorn.
Creche repeats the day's lesson:
"Drake in the lake.
Crow in the wayfaring tree.
Come to me.
Come to me."

At Max Yasgur's Farm, 1969 (Woodstock, N.Y.)

In the Walmart parking lot
one steamy Missouri noon,
a 260-pound, balding woman
wearing a red tasseled top and
short-short shorts,
attempts to separate her sweat-sticky butt
from a hot car seat.

Gripping the burning door frames for leverage,
she spreads her legs for balance,
revealing tattoos,
one each on the pale crepe of her upper thighs:
a blazing sun left,
on the right a crescent moon
tied with pink ribbons.
In my brain's closet,
I glimpse her, a blonde sylph,
wearing a wreath of wilted dandelions and
soggy, blue bachelor's buttons,
dancing in the rain,
wearing sheer panties, mud and giggles.

Her cadaverous friend—
oily locks curveting
around his enameled head
like roan carousel stallions—
twirls and stomps to her rhythm,
jeans thrown under a Farmall.
His rakish paisley headband
reeks of patchouli oil,
as heavenly whispers guide him
to her wet, warm, black hole.

Later, after a lurid sunset,
on the wet stage,
Mary Jane bellows at the top of her lungs.
Sprawled on a painters' tarp,
just outside one of the smoky tents of light
issuing from a host of damp, struggling bonfires,
the unkempt compass of the day
pointed once again
to Heaven.

Maui Sunset

Palms strain sun from sky;
a Ferris of limbs wheels around each hairy trunk
like walking urchin spines.
The fronds lazily sweep and comb
like feeding barnacles,
like the blue fins of black reef fish,
like the electric manes of pin wheeling broncs,
slow and lazy as the sea snake cruising
coarse white sand deep in green canyons.

Creampuff clouds are straight out of Winslow Homer's Bermuda.
White walls, too.
Sun is neon, orange and pink—like reef fish so bright
they make imagination wince,
so brilliant they cannot be recalled after they pass,
like the notes of a sonata on first hearing,
like invisible parrots reflected
in a rainbow arcing above waving cane fields
along the Hana Coast.

Air is warm and moist as surf
strained by coral into froth,
and the irrepressible mynas
quarrel in six languages.
Finally they resort, in the harsh tones of robobirds,
to a guttural exchange in pidgin
as they swoop over pool and perfumed plumerias
to dive on white cake crumbs and green mantises.
Beyond the waterfall,
koi circle, sequined Rockettes.
"We painting," read the painters' shirts
as they gather pails and brushes to go home.
"We painting."

Correspondence

The Poet as the Letter P: Stevens Requests More Prunes

Hartford, October 18, 1941

Dear Taylor:
Here is another job for you: more prunes.
Bribe one of your boys to get on the subway to that greengrocer
we both know so well.
I will pay him subway and 50 cents plus the cost, etc., etc.

It is the right time now for prunes for the winter.
The aesthetic of prunes is variations in the tones of a single taste.
And then there is color.
God, what a thing blue is in a fruit,
especially on a cobalt blue plate or guitar,
the inky iridescence of the wrinkled beast illumined in the varnish.
I enjoy a feast of them most when Elsie is in her peignoir
on a Sunday morning,
with *The Times*, pears and cheese
and the windows full of jasmine yellow light.

I do so love pickled herring at the Waldorf Roof
after an evening at the theater.
But it is the right time *now* for prunes for winter,
and I should like four 5-pound boxes and 25 pounds of apricots.
This is about as much as I am likely to use this winter,
and now you have introduced me to Bee Ritchie,
and I have had stoned prunes, it may even be too much.
I have moreover made a separate deposit with Ritchie.
It seems they dip prunes in chocolate
(a deep, warm up-pouring of milky Swiss),
and in November I expect to receive a boon of those.

Nothing spumoni-colored or hybrid, tell the boy.
Nothing shell-shocked. No slithy toves or spent foil, if you please.
Just virgins standing at attention in their wooden cells,
with nipples poised at both ends, nubile,
peaked for nibbles.

I should rather have them packed in sealed one-pound bags
than the 5-pound boxes, but don't go to any trouble;
I am merely expressing a preference.

I have no big news,
but I am sincerely grateful for your interest and kindness
in these autumnal appetites.
The Japanese catalog was a wonder of its kind.
Very truly yours, WS

A Postcard from Sandburg's Cellar

Flat Rock, North Carolina

Rabelais in red boards,
Whitman in green,
Hugo in ten-cent paper covers.
Here they stand on shelves ...

from Carl Sandburg's *Cornhuskers (1918)*

Cool. Peaceful down here:
Peaceful as a dog dreaming on a barn floor.
Quiet: no distractions
from powdery wind whisking miles of corn tassels.
Visitors can scarcely move among these stacks—
stories in towers right to the rafters.
Sidling past the old furnace,
you glower, hunching your shoulders.

I'm moving in tomorrow.
All I need is a good chaise, a good lamp,
a pork chop sandwich and a wedge of gooseberry pie.
(Even in Illinois now, gooseberries are rare as hen's teeth.)
Maybe a hunk of aged Gouda.

In the towers perch endless stories—murders of hungry crows.
The towers, the stacks of books, resemble zigzag rail fence,
stood on end.
We will speak and sing:
Of the caboose of the Limited
Of Chicago skyscrapers
Of a bayonet covered with rust
Of chimneys, of steel mills
Of blue streamers of wigwam smoke
Of axe handles, rakes, raised fingers
Of haystacks
Of bristling, gleaming spear-handles.

The shapes of things forgotten are here:
Monosyllables
Pain over love
Heart's blood
Babylonian tablets
Rafts of logs
The sinister tower of *Childe Roland*
Wagons circled on the prairie on dark nights
A smart hat on a smart horse
Shenandoah
A full, silver moonrise over the timberline.

There are no bars across the way,
neither gate nor hindrance—
only resinous pine boards stacked to form stiles,
only dozens of shining Amish ladders.
The best time to be here rifling the stacks
is when sleet pounds the 8-foot windows in the study,
when the agile ghost of Muir has climbed a giant spruce
to enjoy the storm,
snacking on crumbs from his pocket.
There is no end to the plan and the clue.

I'm moving in tomorrow—that's Thursday.
Send me a letter.
(Doesn't need to be long.)
We have high majestic fooling going on down here.
We have red hot rivets baptizing girders,
40s babes in yellow cotton sundresses.

We have the world:
We have prairie chickens roasted in red clay;
We have hunger and glory.
We have old longing and new reckoning.
Pronunciamentos.
Did I mention raised fingers? Strawberry sodas?
Crowbars.
Rabelais in red covers—
stories on stories, songs on songs.
Watch it! Duck for that water pipe!

Join me?
Abe and Nancy are here,
Karnak and Canopus.
Say yes!

Estrogen: A Letter

Words are the voice of the heart.
—Confucius

"Yo, girlfriend,
you bitch,
you backstabber, you ingrate.
(I won't say "slut"—
but I'm tempted.)
I thought we were pals, bosom buddies,
BFFs, as teens say.
Now I glimpse your slimy hidden agenda:
You set me up for a really big fall.
In the serene autumn of my life,
you skedaddled near under cover of darkness,
pruning my vocabulary like an apple sucker.
Tongue-tied, stumbling,
I suspected as much,
but now medical research confirms my fear.

"Oh, I could just spit!
Words were my shining weapons, my flow-blue tea set,
my wettest tears,
my arms able to embrace the world.
How dare you, churlish girl!
Silly giggler!
I've given you the best years of my life,
burnt offerings of cramps, ruby crystals
and rose petal candles for your altar,
all that good stuff.
Not to mention:
    stammering before mid-terms
    stained mattresses in several states
    one ectopic pregnancy
    one gall bladder set with hundreds of baroque pearls
    one miscarriage

"You always craved my gingersnaps,
my blonde brownies and rum-raisin cookies.
But don't expect any more care packages,
you ingrate.
This is my final communication.
You'll find my phone unlisted
and my address changed.

"Pig!
Here I am balding,
quite chapfallen (those puppet folds).
I can hear you mutter, crone;
I can hear your annoying open-mouthed breathing.
Go ahead, gloat,
you damn shaggy goat,
you ass.

"Now I'm prosaic as a buzz cut.
Inability to retrieve the right words
frustrates me no end,
infantilizes me.
Maybe we needed a pre-nup.
But enough about you.

"Girl,
you were my chemical muse,
ratcheting up my creativity during ovulation.
Now I'm a gulping bass out of water,
high and dry.
Bitch!
Hang your ugly hair over here so I can yank it."

Peavey: A Letter

Dear Dad,
Is it six years already?
Today I see this one word, *peavey*,
and it brings you back:
your round-shouldered walk,
your clean smell like percale on the line,
your broad grin,
complete with dip of chin toward neck.

I don't need to close my eyes
to see you at the woodlot,
felling birch and pine,
limbing trunks,
using tractor and chain
to snake logs out to the dirt road,
and, then, tipping them into place on the pile.
I hear (I feel through my soles)
the peculiar heavy thunk each green log made
when it found its home in the ragged pyramid.

In your hands, the peavey seemed light as a javelin.
You levered with it like a third arm,
the way you did everything—
unselfconsciously, economically.
There was never a waste of motion.

Nor a waste of words.
Words were "good" washers, shiny wall anchors,
to be stored in tiny drawers in the machine shop,
hoarded.
If I squander them all,
all those steel brads and zinc tar paper tacks,
it won't bring you back.

But two syllables can: pea'vey.

Never waste.
I scowled, scuffing galoshes in the leaf litter,
because we couldn't have a "good" Christmas tree—
a perfect eight-footer, straight as a plumb line.
But, no; those would grow to lumber, to clear boards,
two decades down the road.
You'd shinny up and top out a big tree,
maybe a springy cedar,
and whatever fell those 40 bumpy feet
like a long-dead monkey,
that was it.

Dear Dad,
Words to you were blurry doodles, inexact strokes on paper;
wouldn't water cattle, wouldn't patch a roof.
They deserved to stay where they belonged—
in the *Reader's Digest* vocabulary test
you challenged yourself with once a month.
Words were never what they are to me,
untamed as barn cats,
resonant as the bell
in the Yellow Meeting House steeple.
I used to shinny up a pile of seasoning boards
behind the shop to reach the lowest plum branch:
No one else bothered.
Words were plums to pluck, sniff, polish, bite.

But the woodlot, the big trees, spoke to us both.
The light fell, symphonic, through choirs of feathery limbs:
It called for attentive silence.
And we were closest, silent.

Dear Dad,
It is six years since I stood on that back road on Burns Hill.
Snow fills up the woods again,
where frail Mayflowers guard their pulse beneath.
I watch and listen.

Love,
Toots

Harvest

One Summer Before 1950

I am standing in a hayfield.
Dad passes forkfuls of aromatic hay
up to Grandpa on the wagon.
The load grows.
I see unconsolidated clumps of grass thrown up.
They stick in the stack somehow.
Yet they can be moved, juggled to better position
should the need arise.

How is this possible?
That formless things
should unite with others equally slippery
and thereby gain form, yet retain an individuality?

This possibility and impossibility
has become my whole life,
my work.
Always I stand in prickly stubble,
dizzy with heat, squinting in glare, pondering.

(This scene: as clear as if it were a film
seen yesterday.)

Whalescape

We become rooms for whatever almost is.
It speaks in us, trying.
—"Answers" by William Stafford

I

10 p.m., Barrow, September

A landscape unto itself,
undulating black dunes.
No huddled corpse,
but a reclining rubber Buddha,
a captured continent
that croons "tide flats" to the nose.
A dusky rose, a bayside chapel,
a Gulliver napping among puny gawkers,
a fallen star.
(A fallen star.)

The line snaps twice as they ease her onto the bar,
49 feet of tradition—
Inupiaq heat and light,
pink butter and black meat;
a tail 20 feet wide,
a tongue like a rawhide futon.
(Like a rawhide futon.)

The crew claiming this hoard
clambers aboard the slippery, upturned hull
where they perch, honing cutting spades with steel's kiss.
Toddlers sledding sleek prune hide are shooed away.
Now the first layered slabs of muktuk
are peeled away like turfs,
then towed to one side.
(To one side.)

Suddenly a blade releases a surge of clear fluid
and in the flood a glittering missile form.
A baby leaps into our galvanized midst,
seems to cry out—
a single bleat pierces the stillness.
(A single bleat.)

SOMETHING cries out.
Perhaps it's only a shrill of shock and regret,
a psychic scream,
the instant letdown of my female sorrow.
"My namesake," says a proud whaler,
half turning to the crowd.
The moment is a dream
spotlighted by kliegs.

Amnion sinks into the sand,
and the pale pink cord—a hawser, a dryer exhaust—
is neatly severed.
(Neatly severed.)

With gentle care, the biologist on duty tugs the 5-foot fetus
away from the danger of the flensers' long knives
to document its perfection.
"They breed in March," he offers
to the circle of rapt faces.
The pearl gray calf steams in the 10-degree air
but neither breathes nor stirs.

Forgetting cold feet,
women shoulder forward in sympathy, curiosity;
donkeys at the manger.
"Good eating," says one.
(Good eating.)

I seek communion at the other end of the scene,
between polka-dotted lips.
The bowhead rests on her back and right shoulder,
a serene and languid odalisque
with pinto-spotted flanks.
The phalanx of baleen on her upper jaw
thrusts stiffly into the night—

ten-foot pampas,
black palm fronds,
dark, tapering keys and fringes coated with rime.
Arctic breeze plays them like a wind chime—
a tinkling just audible above the surf,
a siren tune, an icy dirge.
            (An icy dirge.)

II

Noon, the following day

Laboring all night, the crew penetrates to the core.
with hooks they haul forth the minotaur liver—
quivering lobes enough to fill a bathtub.
Body heat threatens the spoils,
scarlet bubbles already boiling around black boots.
The meat is porous—lava boulders.
The blubber is strawberry ice,
darkening in the air to beefy red.
            (Beefy red.)

Now they are felling the black forest,
hacking out plates of baleen
from obdurate stumps.
Freshly ground hatchets swing again and again.
Later they'll clean up the 600 horny slabs—
First pare with a jackknife,
then steel wool, then Mop 'n Glo;
scrimshaw, initial,
Offer to tourists for $10, $12 a foot.
Females have the prettiest hair, they say.
            (The prettiest hair.)

Meanwhile, wheeling gulls keen overhead,
awaiting their turn at the board,
And every yard stacks up its winter hoard,
its alphabet blocks of plenty.
            (Plenty.)

September 15, 12:04 p.m. (Chugiak)

The flowerbeds are mulching themselves under leaves.
My son is in the garden under a yellow umbrella,
choosing a carrot for lunch.

Now he comes to the window waving a whopper.
Now he comes inside smelling like a wet dog.

We crunch together, rabbit hutch:
carrot, lettuce.
Liverwurst next. Peppermint tea.

Pleasant to be in out of the wet,
shelves full of preserves and syrups,
cartons full of potatoes, generator ready for windstorm,
mittens darned.

A moose, his rear hooves projecting over the left side,
cools in a red pickup at the Post Office.
Water scatters diamonds over his rough coat.
Inside the hunter spins the tumbler on his box,
humming.

Shooting Down New Year

Holly and tulip tree, hawthorn and pine.
gum and hackberry hide the stalking gunman.
His shots, booming at regular intervals,
trace the river's bending.
Deer curl lower in the blow down.
The hare dares not twitch in his thicket.
He shoots, the man, at mistletoe
parasitic on oaks.
His bullets give each bunch a biting kiss.
Green trophies bounce on his thighs.
Along the sandbars, along the red clay banks,
he amuses himself in the thin sunlight,
avoiding saw vine, stepping high over nurse logs,
as hawks circle higher and higher.

Owl Chuck (Anchorage)

For Fern as our 25th anniversary approaches

A silver sliver of light slips,
Like the opening chords of *Scherazade*,
Under the drapes.

Sunday afternoon, the end of April,
We were making love
When I heard the first robins of spring in their duet
Outside our window.
I almost stopped and said, “Listen!”
Because I love that moment so—the first robins.
But I could smell the forest on your shoulder,
McHugh Creek where we had just been hiking.
I could smell the whole forest, the whole Chugach
In a thin veneer of paradise,
A robe a micron thick,
A skim of cream on a milk bottle,
A THICK, RICH layer to lick away—
Spruce needles, old aspen leaves and damp duff,
A soft carpet five or six inches deep.
I could inhale
The California red,
The German cheese with its dusting of paprika,
The beef stick.

Under a massive spruce I found white masses of horned owl pellets
Purified by five feet of snow, just flown.
In one pocket I squirreled away a broken leg bone,
A gnawed knuckle, risible.

At home I brought them out in my palm
To show Son No. 2.
“Is that what you two do in the afternoon—look for owl chuck?”
He asks, disbelieving.
“Yup, that’s it,” we grin.
I toss the bones onto the table and let them lie.
We take the rest of the red up to the bedroom.

A silver sliver of light slips,
Like *Scherazade*, under the billowing drapes.
I can smell the forest on your shoulder,
A thin veneer of paradise,
A plush robe, a skim of cream to lick away.

This poem is just what you hear—words;
Just what you see—ink strikes on white.

But consider it shorthand. Transcribe it.
Consider it emanations of heat from sheets.
Consider it spring,
Consider it Canada geese that mate for life,
Consider it light transmissions through overseas cable.
Short and long, short and long, long.
Morse code from a marriage.

Maybe it's only gibberish, gibberish in uneven lines,
A Chinese laundry list.
But pretend it's a cipher for an afternoon in spring
When robins sang and we made love,
When I could smell the whole forest on your skin.
When your body was spruce branches
Sheltering me from the storm coming over Portage.
When resin ran down the trunk we leaned against
Like molten gold.
Consider it ambergris flung up in Turnagain Arm.

To a 16-year-old, it's owl vomit.
"Is that what you two do in the afternoon—look for owl chuck?"
He asks in a rising tone of incredulity.
"Yup, that's it,"
We answer, grinning, glad not to be found out.

I toss the bones onto my placemat and let them lie,
Until we come down later, languid in flannel,
And get on with the business of dinner for the boys.

Now Desire

For my husband on his 42nd birthday

Now desire returns,
even now returns.

It is your skin
that I sink in,
that I think on.
Do my nerves turn to silk,
my fingertips?
Or does your skin?
for that is all I feel

silk, silken skin.
Now desire returns,
even now returns.

Clever as the sun
it rolls along,
rolls,
returns,
desire returns.
Clever as the sun
it rolls from nerve to nerve,
quickening, quick,
quickening, quick.

Like a train it drums,
drums thc temples, drums the groin,
drums and warms,
drums and warms,
quickening, quick,
drums and warms.
Now desire returns,
even now returns.

Water in a cup,
a cup,
in a jug,
a beaded jug,
water on the roof,
the metal roof,
dripping down, rolls, rolls,
runs along the street,
the street,
the silky street.
Clever as the sun
it rolls alone:
cloud, rain,
river, cloud,
it runs along,
rolling, runs,
rolls along.

Silken runs along,
runs along,
silken runs
your skin,
your silken skin—

silk.

Understanding the Oedipus Complex

There is nothing Freudian about it.
Here is a boy
stuck at the level of his mother's crotch
for a year or so.
Of course, he is curious;
of course, he asks,
"How do you pee?"
seeing no familiar exit.
Of course, when you explain
he wants a demonstration.

He says,
"When I am a man
I'll have a cat
and you'll take care of it,
and I'll read in my den."

When you muse on grandchildren,
he says, "You will be *my* mummy"—
meaning the mother of *his* children.
You explain "wife,"
an identity he does not grasp.
He understands only "mother,"
which he has drunk
and inhaled
and bitten
and wet upon from first light.

That's the reason
he separates husband and wife,
worming into every chance embrace,
why he falls off your bed
to distract you
when you kiss Sunday mornings.
That's the reason
he must kiss *you* on the "mouff"
with great smacking kisses.

"Mummy."
"What?"
"Mummy."
"What?"
"Mummy."
"If you want something, say it;
don't say 'Mummy' ten times."
"Mummy."
"What?"
"I love you."

"When I'm a man
and you hear a white dump truck coming,
you'll know it's me.
And we'll go for a ride.
But you can't touch any of the knobs.
And we'll go the Chinese restaurant,
and I won't spill on my shirt."

There is nothing Freudian about it.
No three roads
diverging in a yellow waste.
Just a boy
stuck at crotch-height
and curious about what he faces.

Your name is "Mummy."
You own no other.
When you are going out of an evening,
he whines, "Who will get dinner?"
He knows your place.
He sees it clearly.

What you are, you are, and will be
to him when he's a man.
What does he know of Marcus Aurelius' river—
or growing old?
His life is
peanut butter,
chocolate chip cookies,
white dump trucks.
And Mummy.

Sides-to-the-Middle

Addie Louisa Richardson Fox, my great grandmother,
having digested her sunrise Bible bite,
sat down by the window with a sheet.
(The light was better there.)
The sheet gaped in the middle.
No matter.
Repair:
She scissored it neatly down the center,
trimmed the worn panel away,
brought the outside edges together
and stitched them overhand
twenty stitches to the inch.
They call it sides-to-the middle.

If you want to define "land poor,"
look at this sheet.
If you want to define "thrift" or "mending,"
consider this sheet.
If you want to define "pride,"
behold this sheet.

When the center was whole,
Addie Louisa Richardson Fox
hemmed the new sides.
Then she tatted a wide lace for the top,
applied it, and topped off the lace with
a matching ribbon of linen.
They call it sides-to-the-middle.

This sheet has traveled from Massachusetts
to California to Alaska to North Carolina—
has seen more of the world than great-grandmother did.
No matter.
Now frost threatens the new weeping cherry tree,
and knowing Addie's love of cherries,
I pull out the sheet.
I staple it over the mouse-ears of green.
It flaps in the wind: a vanilla lollipop.

A week later, the tree blooms.
If you want to make Addie's acquaintance,
come see my blooming cherry.
I call it Sides-to-the-Middle.

Subdivisions

Based on Larry Heath's Cutting Tin & Cake, *metal and paint, Hickory Museum of Art, North Carolina; 2013.*

Your recipe for art:
Take one sheet of recycled tin.
Snip and rotate and fold into a leafy dome of trees,
a kite rising white before an orange moon,
a sandy children's playground, a trio of herons
safely screened from two outdoorsmen in a canoe.
Keep cutting from broad trunks until
you spin your way to the finest branch ends
or threads of grass.

Amazing feat:
subdivision of a two-dimensional sheet
into a sculpture that stands alone
in three dimensions. Apply a trace of paint,
chemical jelly, a ball peen, some heat
or discreet burnishing—Voila! a peaceful scene.

Here you bend into being two men seated at a table.
The third friend is a dog, being petted
by the extended hand
of the man in the white cap.
The men savor a picnic of delicious talk.
Frilled butterflies draw near,
drink their fill.

Your mother subdivided your face
by binding her belly
to hide your presence.
But you were able to reverse all that unloving,
all that cursed folding, molding, tucking of your limbs.
You found your way home
through the grace of creativity.
The transformation is all.

The House that Bias Built

"That's how we feed the animals."
—Two men at the 2012 Republican Convention explaining why they are throwing peanuts at an African-American camerawoman

"If I had a son, he would look like Trayvon."
—President Barack Obama

This is the house that bias built.

This is the watchman
who skulked in the house that bias built.

This is the teen out for a walk
who chanced near the watchman
who skulked in the house that bias built.

These are the sweets that tempted
the teen out for a walk
who chanced near the watchman
who skulked in the house that bias built.

These are the merchants
who sold the sweets that tempted
the teen out for a walk
who chanced near the watchman
who skulked in the house that bias built.

This is the lust for sales and profit
that prompted the merchants
who stocked the sweets that tempted
the teen out for a walk
who chanced near the watchman
who skulked in the house that bias built.

This is the crop that needed cheap labor
that fed the lust for sales and profit
that prompted the merchants
who stocked the sweets that tempted
the teen out for a walk
who chanced near the watchman
who skulked in the house that bias built.

This is the trade in flesh and blood
that tends the crop that needed cheap labor
that fed the lust for sales and profit
that prompted the merchants
who stocked the sweets that tempted
the teen out for a walk
who chanced near the watchman
who skulked in the house that bias built.

These are the shadows of whip and chain
that haunt the fields and cloud men's brains
as they gnash the flesh and blood
that tends the crops that need cheap labor
that fed the lust for sales and profit
that prompted the merchants
who stocked the sweets that tempted
the innocent teen who donned a hoody
to go out for a walk
who chanced near the watchman
who skulked in the house that bias built.

This is the cycle that we must end,
to erase the shadows of whip and chain
that haunt fields and alleys and cloud men's brains
as they consume the flinching flesh and blood
of slave labor that tends those crops that need cheap labor
that fed the lust for sales and profit
that prompted the merchants
who stocked the Skittles that tempted
innocent Trayvon who donned a hoodie
for his walk in the dark,
Trayvon who chanced near the watchman
who carried a gun and
skulked in the house that bias built.

Driving Black

How wonderful it is that nobody need wait a single moment
before starting to improve the world.
—Anne Frank

Use a light foot.
Keep your eyes open.
Mind the signs.
Don't drive a white convertible.
Shun the shades.
Shun the gun.
You'll be stopped anyway.

When stopped:
No smirks.
No one-liners.
Hustle uppity words underground.
Conceal your muscular butt in ruffles.
Leave gaudy jewelry on the dresser.
Ditch the do-rag.
Shave the soul patch.
You'll be stopped anyway.

When stopped:
Conceal your education.
Mute gestures as well as tone.
Meat steams on the table,
but no place is set for you.
Never an open door, never a glass of wine.
Take anything for granted:
quicker than boiled asparagus,
you'll be stopped.

Fling the bling.
Smoke no toke.
Feign no brain.
Heed the speed.
Scorn the horn.
Bag the rag.
Scratch the patch.
Shed the dreads.
Pass on sass. Ignore the crass.
Odds are, you'll be pulled over.

Mary Porter Is Carried from the Morning Star Baptist Church in Mattapan

Carnell Porter was twenty-nine,
Doing fine.
Now he's dead,
Shot once in the head.

At Morning Star, men and babies cried
Because Carnell had died.
The All God's Children Choir sang.
Dusty rafters rang.
Notes blossomed true,
Spilling onto Blue Hill Avenue.

Mary Porter rose to her feet.
In a dream she moved, in the awful heat.
She clawed at the velvet, white and gray.
Blue carnations seemed to sway.
"Oh, my baby, my baby.
My good little boy."

Being black is a full-time job.
Carnell hated violence; hated mobs.
Ten ushers in white gloves looked real swell.
Ten Red Cross nurses caught Mary as she fell.

Mary Franklin sang.
Ancient rafters rang.
Notes spilled across the aisle
Like mourners, single file.

Woodgate and Woodbole, by and by,
Corbet Street Gang getting high.
The Man came, didn't care.
Then Carnell chanced there.

Gang kicked the car Carnell was in.
"What's the problem?" Carnell said,
Just the shadow of a frown,
But polite; Mary taught him right.
They gunned him down.
"No justice at all," said Uncle Ernest,
Straightening the pall.

Carnell Porter was twenty-nine
English High grad, doing fine.
Now he's dead,
Shot once in the head.

Ten Red Cross nurses stood in a row,
Ten white caps bending low.
They caught Mary Porter as she fell down,
Stained-glass light her Sunday crown.

Trumpets and horns rose like a prayer
As Mary was shouldered from there.
"Evil all around," said the reverend.
"Carnell was a sheep among wolves."
"Amen" echoed down the aisle
Single file.

Melvin rose to say farewell.
He kissed cold Carnell.
"Goodbye, brother.
Goodbye, my brother," Melvin said
To his brother lying dead.

Being black is a full-time job.
Carnell hated violence; hated mobs.
Ten ushers in white gloves lent a hand
To bear Mary Porter into the glare of Mattapan.

"What's the problem?" asked Carnell.
"Evil all around," said the preacher.
"Carnell was an innocent," said another speaker.
"Evil all around," said the preacher.
"This is not the end," sobbed a friend,
Looking vexed.
"We're next."
"Evil all around," said the preacher.
"Oh, my baby, my baby,
My good little boy."

Carnell Porter was twenty-nine,
Worked with computers, doing fine.
Now he's dead,
Shot once in the head.
"Oh my baby, my baby,
My good little boy."

Howl for Edo

With apologies to Lassie, Timmy, and Allen

I

I am sitting with Edo in his last moments—

Edo, our "Doge,"
our nine-year-old "baby dog,"
who as a pup gained five pounds a week
who has shared our adventures
who knows I am upset during these final minutes and has been muzzled
    for menacing the vet
who greeted me by taking my wrist gently in his jaws
who knew twenty-five words including "in"
who was teased by squirrels at Gull Rock
who loved drinking from icy Chugach creeks
who slept between us in our tent in March below Flattop
who slept most quietly as wolves came within thirty feet of the tent
who if busted in his pubic beard was mon-orchid
who roared like a lion
who would roar now but for the muzzle.

Our "Doge"
who treated our sons as litter mates
who is an Akita, a breed notorious as "serial cat killers"
who knew twenty-five words including "fish"
who delighted in chasing white ptarmigan in white drifts but never
    caught one
who patrolled the sun porch like a general on a hill
who had to be sat on as we pulled quills from his tongue
who wanted to pursue the watching porky as soon as the last quill
    was out
who hugged by leaning his weight against my legs
who relished salmon and beef heart and steak bones
who was in his element in snow, at zero
who was spooked by suspension bridges along Chilkoot
who was as stubborn as his owners

who perched on the toe of your boot so he could see over the gunnels
  the current denizen struggling on the line
who yearned to dive overboard to join the sea lions
who knew twenty-five words including "lion"
whose 108 pounds moved graceful as a gazelle
who enjoyed hanging his tongue, pink laundry, out the car window in
  the breeze
who did not like people whom he did not like
our "Doge" who danced with us in the rain outside our tent
who was forbidden our bed but left secret footprints on the sheets when
  we were at the office
who wrestled with us on the carpet like a pup
who nipped at our ears but never broke the skin
who knew twenty-five words including "bath"
who charmed Japanese cruise ship passengers who threw down candy
  and snapped photos
who looked reprovingly at us when attacked by loose dogs while he was
  restrained by his leash
whose ears were grey plush
whose tail was Cyrano's plume
whose legs were like pillars hewn from cedars of Lebanon
whose undercoat floated like dandelion seeds when he shed
who did not like people whom he did not like
and does not like vets—especially now
who knows I am upset although he doesn't know why
and who still stands after three fatal shots
whose name arose in crossword puzzles
who hated walking in the rain
who knew twenty-five words including "wipe"
who patrolled the sun porch like a Buckingham sentry
who an hour ago on his last walk, allowed off-leash to romp in the snow,
was too sick to play but hugged me for the opportunity anyway
who is a lion to the last, protecting me
who begins to wobble
our "Doge."

II

Moloch is the strange beast off-leash who attacks from behind.
Moloch is the growl and lunge.
Moloch is the suffering.
Not bang nor whimper,
but the sliding of ragged claws on tile, the folding of knees.
Lacklove and muttless in Moloch.

III

The animal hospital illuminates itself.
Canines in their cubicles sing sweet blues.
Holy the pet!

SELECTED POEMS

The Wife & Other Poems (1976)

The Wife

Sitting on her desire,
which throbbed like an alarm clock,
the wife tried to concentrate on *Time*.
Or standing on it,
a white square in a ring of black ones
dappling the supermarket produce aisle,
artichokes and Muzak tugging at her panties,
she tried to decipher a suddenly meaningless list:
squash,
ammonia,
tuna fish,
nutmeg.

But the task was hopeless.
Like Venus,
cursed with a new (over-starched) hymen each bedding,
each time rising from the teeming foam
stunned by the glare of pink fluorescent on bath oil,
fumbling with a ragged towel,
curious and tentative and eager,
bored with limp green salad
and ready for beef and bone,
she wished for any lover
(eel, limber newel post)—
panting but tongue-tied,
perversely puritanical—
not wanting to disturb the man of the house,
reading or away at work.
Her leisure was a turnip
she'd sat on unintentionally
(it unseen nestling in folds of gray nylon upholstery).
It was uncomfortable, unfilled.

Drunk with lust,
wondering where her legs had gotten to—
and who owned these numb stumps in Earth shoes?—
nerve ends perused
the electric bliss of skin on skin.
Her thoughts were light as gull bone;
her anchoring limbs, ponderous armoires.

Emotion changes direction like the wildebeest—
precipitately as a well-oiled hinge.
But action must not.
Unlike the (male) volcano, the wife pussyfoots,
and, if traditionally quiescent,
cannot, without risking comment, suddenly erupt
in a shower of lava bombs and molten rock,
oozing phosphorescent into a hissing sea.
(Pity sex, that fumarole,
left in a silk-lined basket on our doorsteps:
without a country!)

Aware of the body and its functional decorations
(moldings and cornices)—
no fig leaf doilies in *this* living room—
she peered blankly at her magazine,
an empty hive with dreams of bees.

Aubade in International Orange

Camped below Greenleaf Hut
where the rough trail dips slightly
into scrub, a thousand feet
below Lafayette's rocky summit, I start
awake, sandwiched between

slices of damp sleeping bag.
It's nearly dawn and almost raining.
Wind and rabbits rustle the
stunted firs. Overhead the nylon
tent, black-orange in the

half-light, weeps an orange mist.
I twist from one uncomfortable posi-
tion to the next, wincing
when flesh grazes the bag's icy zipper.
Just a few more stiff-jointed

cat naps before booted Aurora
(a buxom, pigtailed Canadienne wearing
Lederhosen, double-knit knee socks,
and an Uncle Sam surplus parka
bloused over a Lafuma rucksack)

strides up the trail on the
run-down heels of the dew. My stomach
mumbles, dreaming of breakfast. By
afternoon we'll be backpacking that
steak knife, Franconia Ridge.

Gram: Only the Ashes

Butterfly! These words
From my brush are not flowers...
Only their shadows
—Soseki

I

Your words:
Outlandish
A beeline
Thunder jug
Calling cards (what mice leave)
Bound and determined
By guess and by gory ("by hook and by crook")
Tea kettle
Stuffing (for "dressing")
Supper ("dinner") dinner ("lunch")
Garden Special (tomatoes stewed with celery and onion; canned)
Overtown ("downtown")
Thunderstruck ("surprised")
Waist ("blouse")
About ready to jump out of my skin ("nervous, anxious").
Light somewhere.
The wreck of the Hesperus [a mess].
Don't be so provoking!
I don't know what possessed him!
Procrastination is the thief of all time.
It's a dirty bird shits in its own nest.

Your flowers:
iris
peony
lily of the valley
bee balm (to lure hummingbirds)
coral bells
tiger lilies
lilac
Spirea Vanhouttei
wisteria

forsythia.
Pig weed, bind weed thistles, nettles, witch grass:
even these are yours by virtue of the time you spent
wrenching them out.

Your familiars:
horse cars
soapstones
dogs, puppies, cats, kittens
tailor's chalk
needle books, darning eggs, buttonhole twist
mittens
rocking chairs
Finnan Haddie
roast chicken with stuffing
pork with applesauce
dandelion greens and Swiss chard
gingersnaps
Boston Cream Pie
apple turnovers
flannel nightgowns
bloomers
slips
a straw hat trimmed with wheat and brown grosgrain ribbon
aprons that match your dresses
ironing boards
sleeve boards
steamer trunks
doorstops
spading forks
hair nets
jar rubbers
lists, rags, string
worry, faith, good deeds

I asked you once how you could be so calm
when awful things happened,
and you burst out, "My angel mother,"
meaning your foster mother, "Aunt Stella."
She had been such a good example
of equanimity in the face of sorrow.

II

A grandson in basic training addresses his letters to "Ethyl";
but almost everyone— including your son— calls you "Gram."
Your grandsons' friends "Hi, Gram"
as they make a beeline from front door to cookie jar.
You are one of those who give "shape and substance to our
national character."

III

Since you turned eighty—
wishing myself the ant, able to make twenty observations a second—
I've been trying to get you down on paper,
before grief drowns order and time shuts the door on memory.
Notes pile up,
but still I'm nowhere;
You elude me like a wraith, a witch . . . .
I sit here in my flannel nightgown and hear myself
saying to my three-year-old,
"Light somewhere!" as he circles the couch for the ninth time.

The thought of losing you is so unbearable that I
must fix you on paper before you migrate:
like trying to paint a Monarch from life
as it flits from milkweed blossom to pink milkweed blossom.
pursuing I leave a trail of unfinished sketches,
index cards ("never heard of Rbt. Frost, but an encyclopedia of tatting"),
and squashed tubes of pigment.
In your life there's no order but necessity,
and finally I borrow that.
These are fragments shored against your flight,
and my sorrow.

A visit to a Bay Area cemetery:
the horror of cobwebbed coffins stacked in a crumbling monument
behind corroded bars and glass bulls-
eyed by bb's,
an inscription ("only the ashes"),
urns missing from cornices,
rubble and green slime in flowerpots,

a mysterious suitcase overturned
and strewn with framed photos and daguerreotypes
on the dirty floor of a granite mausoleum,
picture medallion gouged from headstone of "beloved infant."
These spur my poem, light my tiny lamp for the bestial dark.
These and your handwriting,
growing more erratic each letter.

IV

Your anecdotes:
The one about seeing "the little goldy cloud" drift from
the upper window of a house where an old man lay ill;
reaching home, you learned he had died.
(You had me type this up for *Reader's Digest*, but they declined to print it.)

The one about the lady desirous of proving herself a Yankee in true
Mayflower Descendants and DAR fashion;
she zealously delved into her ancestry back to 1770—
to find a Tory.

The recent one about filling the dog's dish with dry meal
and next morning finding the toes of your shoes rattling with it; mice
had tediously carried it there
for safekeeping.

These (and others) unpretentiously but with zest and purpose.

V

I have seen her
~ angry because a local newspaper falsified a story for sensational
effect
~ bent like a peasant putting stones on strawberry runners
~ accompany me, as her birthday present, to a movie to which I
(at eleven) had won two passes in a newspaper coloring contest
(the thought not occurring to me for years that perhaps she
didn't care for westerns!)
~ try six times to thread a needle before asking me
~ read and summarize with relish (at eighty-one) a science fiction novel
about a second Ice Age
~ smile at a jonquil
~ dice celery into a bowl when there was nothing else for salad
~ cut a Baldwin into eighths against her thumb (crosshatched with
seventy years of apples) to eat with sharp Cheddar
~ crack butternuts all afternoon to get enough for one batch of cookies
(forbidden in her own diet)
~ intently follow TV soap operas
~ fret over the unprotected places cats choose to have kittens
~ shudder at six a.m. as she struggled to inject insulin into
a crepey thigh
~ mocked by grandchildren too young to understand age's mental
hesitations
~ save everything that could possibly be of future use
~ pitied by 5 & 10 clerks as we shopped together overtown, they
unaware how
Spirit sings unflagging in a shuffling body
~ shorten her dresses an inch and a half in deference to the mini skirt
era, so that her hems reached a scant inch below her knees

I have never seen her:
~ comfortable with leisure
~ drink alcohol or cry (but have seen her so emotional at visiting her
husband—from whom she has been separated 20 years—that
she seized his nearer hand and shook it, giggling soundlessly)
~ chafe at the bit of the inevitable or sudden

~ swear or lie or libel (but I winced at her outrage once when she said
to my brother, who had been spreading exaggerated reports of
Dad's divorce, "It's a dirty bird shits in his own nest." She
repeated the proverb; her tone would have cowed Huns.)

VI

Her teachings:
reticence
endurance
honor
patience
thrift
humor
forbearance
tact.
(These exemplified not stated.)

VII

Her life:
Orphaned at nine.
Separated from her siblings but given to
kind foster parents,
"Uncle" a tailor.
Earned $2 a day sewing in private homes.
Married at twenty-five,
her small waist set off by a brown suit and real beaver hat;
the town gave her a surprise shower.
A happy union.
(Once she reminisced *her* husband shunned pajamas, too.)
Lost two sons,
the first a blue baby of a few days,
the second of jaundice at three months.
Advised not to try again but persisted.
Had a healthy daughter with a full head of black ringlets.
Walked a mile in 1920 to a neighboring farm to buy an egg,
because the marvelous child hadn't had one in ten days;
The egg cost a dime.

Son two years later.
His pet lamb, Mary, would follow him into the house
            and upstairs.
Then the accident in '32.
Grandpa parked his truck and was getting out.
A loaded truck out of control sprang down the hill
facing and engaged.
A buttonhole caught on the key in the ignition
stopped Dad from bursting on the sidewalk like a water balloon;
he bedded down on the hood with gashes.
After two weeks of coma Grandpa roused and said
to Gram, vigilant at the bedside,
"Did I cash Aunt Stella's check?"
(She had had a premonition, had begged him not to go
to market that day; she is not one to beg.)
Things were never the same.
Grandpa lost all gumption.
Dad assumed the chores in high school,
giving up the idea of law.
The daughter (after college, art school, job in NYC)
was embittered by paralysis n '50.

Enduring:
Years of drought
Fire in the windbreak past the barn
Land poverty
Diabetic shock at seventy
A disabled daughter in the house
A divorced son with five children in the house
Cataracts in both eyes.
At eighty had to switch from pills to shots again.
When weight melted away she found she had no breasts,
simply creases; this amused her.

VIII

As More valued God
more than his king or his neck,
so she values others.
She steeps care
as water infuses tea.

IX

The clump of yolks diminishing into infinity as she
cleans a chicken.
The soul thrives on contrast.
Restoration's cricket chirrups at my ear.

For Ethel Kimball Bodwell Fox, 1888-1979.

Love in Mother Lode Country

Mercury flushed gold
as hounds tree raccoons.
Now grouse in their mating dance scoot like taxiing planes.
Snow dusts granite peaks.

Placer gold's the easiest to glean:
free-dust, dull-yellow flakes,
and nuggets like petrified peas
washed down from the hills in the Rush
and erosion's rape.
Men still sift pans of black sand,
dripping with the milk of silt from spring's cataracts.

Metaphors glint among gravel.
I live with a dried pea between my thighs the better
to hold love's precious dust—
as merchants
once indented weighing thumbs.

At Tincup, Fairplay, Lulu City, Eureka,
Bonanza, Climax, Tarryall, Skull Creek,
at Rough and Ready, Angels Camp, Copperopolis,
Chinese Camp, Placerville,
love's the ore we mine for.
sifting through lascivious intentions,
playing at pleasantness—
behind huge, megaphoned masks
(faces of tolerance, sensitivity, complacence
humor, intelligence, good nature); love's
that glitter in the clearing wash,
the still point at the center of turning,
the point between motion and stasis
kinetic sculpture seeks.

These golden balls on strings, probing inclined planes,
these cutout Lucite sheets shifting in frames,
these magnetized, polished bronze cubes—
all seek a certain angle of repose,
of hip on hip, of thigh on thigh.

Adoption

To Alex, twenty-three months

Two Jehovah's Witnesses in navy blue suits
come up the road,
frightening you,
and you run
to put your face
in my crotch for solace.

You didn't come out of me,
but you keep going in.
Your smiles,
your bubbling laughs,
your falling over, delighted, with a new word,
your sidelong glance and
chin on clavicle
when you know you're being observed—
they go into me like knives.

Your whole muscular body goes soft as
a cinnamon bun sometimes.
Across the room
I see your softness.
Your face is a down parka.
The softness sinks in, into me.

Your timidity is mine,
is me as a child.
You put on my past like a parka.
You put on my long eyelashes,
the gleaming satin nape of my neck.
You put on my soft baby feet,
my tender earlobes.

I hold myself by the hand
as the barking dog circles,
as the bush planes roar over,
the strange men come closer.

When I must rinse dirt from your eye,
I am the one screaming
upside down under the gushing faucet.
As the lump rises on your lip,
I hug myself.

Nice knives.
Come cut me up.

The Island

"He was being drawn away by a force like a high wind, yet smooth and silent."
—Watership Down

In the tiny bedroom
the bed is
ringed with shoals
of books—
library,
borrowed,
bought.
The kids think it's
a football field,
a trampoline.
On Sunday mornings,
we have to shoo them off,
hooting like savages
after wild pigs
in a rain forest.

The sheets cost too much;
they put washing machine loads
out of balance,
sending off alarms.
The violet comforter is mortgaged.

No man is an island,
but friends in a King size bed are—
barricaded with reefs of
cast off clothing,
with shoe coral.

Somewhere in the
dark room under the bleachers,
the atomic bomb is being discovered,
and Hazel-rah
tries to speak Lapine to
a dust-kitten.

Crime and Punishment
gives you
nightmares.
Field & Stream
gives me a new
market.
Playboy gives us
ideas.

On the warm sands
3000 years of Chinese poetry
grapple with
Computer Power and Human Reason.
The Mother Knot
lassoes the
Sears catalog.
Redbook tells a short, short story
to *House & Garden.*
Noshing on breadfruit,
Bambi has his tender consciousness
raised by *Galaxy.*
Henry Gemmill interviews
Nora Ephron
who interviews
Abbie Hoffman.
A lesser ape straight out of *National Geographic*
swings from a clotheshorse.
The New Yorker
makes notes and comments.
The latest brochure
from the Zucchini Advisory Board
buys a beer for a seed germination chart.
Jean Shepherd describes a Hupmobile
to Sanche de Gramont.

Pillows shed
feathers around
our nest.

Somewhere in the nest of this cozy room,
you kiss my
Dewey Decimal System.

The Wife: Part II (1979)

Notes on Speech

A series of haiku chronicling my older son's learning to speak.

(1) Walking/Skating

Thud—the toddler sprawls
on the open *Mother Goose's*
words—slippery as ice.

(2) His First Word

"What was his first word—
'Mummy' or 'Daddy,'?" they ask.
"Dog," we have to say.

(3) The Zoo at 16 Months

Moos like a cow, caws
like a crow, growls like a bear—
and won't say a word.

(4) Eighteen Months

Yves points, asks, "Uh? Uh?"
"Airplane," we say. "Uh?" "Airplane."
This goes on for months.

(5) His First Sentence

At eighteen months can
sit through a whole book. His first
sentence: "Mum, read book."

(6) Yves's First Popcorn

White blossoms open;
Yves (two years, two months) shouts from
his stool, "Peacocks' tails!"

(7) Climbing up Dah's Leg

Yves (three years, four months)
says, "I climb you like a lit-
tle river." He sits.

(8) Goals at 3 ½

Planning ahead, Yves
declares, "When I grow up, I'll
be an elephant."

(9) At the Checkout Counter, 43 Months

"What's in those cans, Mum?"
"Antifreeze," I say.
"It's for ants?" Yves asks.

(10) Yves at 44 Months

Describing a bath-
robe fringe: "It's a thread, Mum, and
it has lots of friends."

(11) Perception at 44 Months

At the exit of
a wet blanket, Yves cheers, "Now
we can be alive."

(12) Sibling Rivalry at 45 Months

"Ma, what you doin'?" "I'm
changing Alex." "What Alex?" Yves
asks quite straight-faced.

(13) The Nancy Drew Fan, Almost 5

Pushing a Tonka
outside, shouts: "Look, Al, a clue—
a stolen footprint!"

(14) Just 5, Playing Games with Younger Brother

"Dwarf, get my candy,
my magic TV, and my
gold. That will cheer me."

(15) Dreaming, Just 6

Hearing fear, I rush
in. "Yves!" "It's OK, reading
a new book of rhymes."

Hard Candy

I

"Pain, pain!" you shriek,
smashing your palms against your skull
as if violence could relieve.

Nothing could have been worse
than seeing you
wheeled from minor surgery,
swollen lips shiny with blood and Vaseline,
adenoidal blood caking your nostrils,
eyes furious, weary, betrayed.

Nothing except this:
having to administer drops
to clear the ear bobbins of protein.
The drops burn.
(We can't tell you we must do this
twice again, tomorrow.)

II

Left from the holidays:
Bitter orange mummies—
or are they Santas?—
the molds eroded by sugar.
Red-and-white striped peppermint drops,
Green-and-white wintergreen sticks,
lumpish yellow ornaments,
hard pillows of peanut butter.

You try one and are confused—
spoiled by years of marshmallow and
yielding chocolate.
"Suck," we urge. "It takes
a long time to eat.
Just let it melt in your cheek."

You give up after one,
too much work.
(I dissolve the rest with hot water
and throw the mess on the compost.)

III

It's all hard candy, son.
Takes too much work,
takes too long,
hurts.

"Throw them away!" you scream,
wanting the evidence gone
now the last evil deed's done.
(The bottle of drops
hits the trash
with a sweet thud.)

Building a Fire in the Rain (The Sierra)

At 3000 feet,
clouds drift from the next canyon
and overwhelm the trail.
We pitch camp in the rocky cirque.
Rain pours down.
Our backs are damp,
but not our appetites.

Deep in my marrow
one gene lurks
that knows how to build fires
in the rain.
It sniffs out dry grass
at the base of spruce trunks.
It turns over wet logs
to find dry punk.
It stuffs its pockets with bark.
I exult as the smoke rises,
dark and wet at first,
then light and hot,
as the eggs scramble,
the tea steeps.

Marriage is like this:
years of rain,
shortages of tact and hard cash.
But for this
I have no genes to cope.
At home we both fall apart,
having spent all patience elsewhere.
Neuroses (like light)
play tricks:
We hear what no one said,
feel what no one meant,
suspect,
suspect.
Spirits dampen.

The rain pours down.
Hail falls onto the Spam
and dehydrated potatoes.

Days when I stink of
Varathane and jam,
how can I respond
to your kitchen goosings?
Days when you stink
of office politics,
how can you respond to mine?
How to rekindle the flames
of romance?
(Dry spruce cones are not enough.)

Are we meant to go beyond,
to hike through the flames
into another canyon,
a place of banked coals?

Do we try to revive the past
in the camp of the future?

I do not know.
I puff on green alders;
smoke fills my lungs;
tears fall like rain.

Ptarmigan Valley: Poems of Alaska (1980)

Van Cliburn Among the Crowberries

Centuries of moss sing here
in mellow green hummocks,
the soft mastabas of forgotten berries,
multiple inviting buttocks
of earth.
Here the crowberries
twine their green inviting tendrils,
as the creek descends
through damp alders.

Here near the sky
all but rock is miniaturized:
birch are but a leafy handspan;
valleys, a yard square.

Giants in this landscape,
we gambol among the hummocks
devouring the inhabitants;
our blue-lipped children
roll down upholstered slopes
laughing like tumbleweeds.

Big hands come into their own here,
rippling the fruited valleys
like keyboards,
cascading black berries
into harmonious pails—
a whole pastorale of pies.

Ptarmigan Valley

Gargoyles frightened men toward heaven;
pitchy devils on ladders leered and
brandished dripping pitchforks.
In Ptarmigan Valley,
my ghost (light as the mallard feather on
Mirror Lake) floats aloft,
skimming the spruce-tops like a fisher,
and comes to rest in a rose bush,
top-heavy among the airy fireweed.

Up the mountain.
in the six-foot grass,
the she-bear suckles her twins,
while her mate mumbles over a
chaw of stiff moosehide
under a cottonwood half a mile away,
scattering hair in a huge circle.

So quiet. The burner under the tea water
is mistaken for a woodpecker,
and the water pump sounds like
Doomsday.
The crisp mutterings
of the birch logs on the fire,
the clock on the mantel,
coyotes howling in the foothills,
my neck chafing my collar, my pen scratching,
these are the only sounds of this September night.

No devils here.
Perfection nudges me heavenward.

The Walrus Come to Gambell in the Spring

Milk white
sun beats down on
ice. The young cow rakes
a flipper to shade her eyes; her
calf sucks.

Egg packed
in an icebox,
ungainly walrus stabs
mumbling walrus with his sharp tusks:
"Back off!"

Man comes in oomiak.
A senior bull sounds his
warning bell, and the pod slips from
the floe.

Below,
whales sing sonar
chorales, convoluted
spirals curling to ice ridges
and back.

Weightless,
ivory rakes
the sand, churning up clams,
snails, cockles. The calf hitches rides
on Ma.

Sonatina: Inukshuk

We groped for stones beneath the mud—
The legs are rarest, being long;
We scraped the seeds of ice, the eggs
Of snow, the sheer Miocene crud
From the flat surfaces. Along
The ridge mists hammered their tent pegs
And settled down to watch. "Rock thud
On peg," said Kokeok, "like song
Of ice at sunset, stretching legs
For sea so we go hunt oogruk.
Hand me the head." At last the arms
Held, beckoned, embraced. Would he work
His art again this year? Skin charms
Were tucked beneath cold ribs; we stayed
To tea up in his lee and pray.

Woods (Lowell)

Black footscraper on granite stoop
stands guard for
white clapboard,
Whistler's Home,
where his Mother—
what the artist called
"Arrangement in Grey and Black"—
does not appear even in print.

Distant kin to Jim
(imperious butterfly),
my eye declares
the shades of woods
filling up with snow
are palette enough for
fifty artists.
The flow of colors
relaxes;
the slow glide
of flakes is an oiled
caress.

In Lowell, where his home looms,
woods fill up, too, as they do
here in Chugiak beyond my sink.
Snow dapples alders into rabbit fur.
Crotches of birches
and arms of spruce
gather a white weight,
while their own bulk
grows blacker
as the shadows grow,
until they fill
up that cup
of mountains,
night.

On a Human Scale

This close to the green sea,
wild geraniums and Nootka lupine all around,
one does not need cathedrals
to see God.

God humbles Himself;
He walks among the white crosses
on the bluff,
among the graves nodding with chocolate lilies,
buys Pepsi and sunglasses
at the general store,
cuts bait for halibut,
stands in stench and gum boots
smashing crabs on the cannery wedge.

The three bulb domes loom above the hill
as He trudges up the path from Ninilchik,
loom like a three-master at anchor
in a bay surrounded by gentle hills
green and white with Indian celery.
A ladder stands ready against the clapboard;
the archpriest mounts the homely rungs
to ring out worship.

Narrow white room where men
can stand only five abreast,
and God must bow His head
as He enters.

Grizzly

To conquer nature is to commit suicide.
—from The Frisco Kid, Jerry Kamstra

The baby won't go to anyone but me.
But he went to the zookeeper, rode on his shoulders,
went behind the fence with him, almost nose to nose
with the blonde grizzly.

"Watch this," said the grinning keeper (who had
just been wrestling Binky, the polar bear).
He crouched and hopped.
The blonde, all 700 half-grown pounds,
crouched and hopped.
They hopped in sync the length of the cage front;
then turned, repeated.

Back home I said to the baby
(building up his memory cells),
"Remember the bear?"
He crouched and hopped for answer.
His coat rippled in the wind like wild oats,
wild oats.

Trapper

It will come if it is there and if you will let it come.
—Gertrude Stein

"Got my method from an expert,
a sourdough
who once downed four caribou
with one bullet.
Said they walked into that little canyon
single file, neat as you....

"You hang a rag of moosehide
from a limb with a string.
And you use a rusted trap.
(It has no human-scent.)
You scatter shredded bark
over the trap,
and hope for snow to fall
on top of that.
A sharpened pencil is best.

"And then you pray.
And you pace in your cabin
(roasting a caribou haunch, maybe),
and usually the furry lines
are intrigued by that bit of rag,
twisting in the wind off the glacier,
and get caught in your trap.

"If they're not dead
when you arrive with the dogs,
you finish them off
with a dose of revision."

The Ermine

The baby disappears behind the white drapes
with unusual zest,
and following him I see
the ermine.

Dazzling, white as milk,
it cavorts on the drifted lawn
(suddenly raised to the peerage).
Shoulders cloaked in white light
eyes like jet beads,
tail dipped in an inkwell,
it explores
footsteps, moose prints, mouse holes,
pouring itself into crevices:
furred liquid.

Thus our November morning
appears,
pouring itself sinuously
onto this white page
tipped with black ink.
(This final period's its nose.)

Allego

On the south Baffin coast, in the winter of 1913-14, Robert Flaherty, called Koodjuk (swan) because of his white skin, is photographing the Eskimos (Inuit). The woman, Allego, is his helper. She subsequently becomes a famous shaman. Nanook of the North *was filmed six years later.*

Too cold for writing on paper,
so we used flat stones.
We mist them with our breaths,
then scribe with driftwood.
Chinook melts our messages,
like fox prints on the beach.
Only Emenik and I do this;
Koodjuk taught us.

I help him in the little house.
Women think it funny
to nail up wet sealskins
on the outside while we work.
Sometimes as we wait,
prints melting into view
in their stinking sea
(seals rising at blow holes),
children think it funny
to open the door a crack,
laugh, slam it, run off.
They try to bother us with light.
(Children do not know
I have strung up a caribou rug
on a line, to block their tricks.)

Avaleeniatuk, who starved to death,
surfaces today.
He is out with his dogs even now.
His three children are not even born.
But I know he and they will starve
and freeze ten winters hence.
The black seaweed
whispers this.

My face is smooth now,
smooth as my braids.
But soon I journey north.
They tattoo me there—
magic lines,
the spirits' beautiful script.
My powers rise in me slowly,
like the tide.
They seep in
while lie in Swan's arms,
though I shall not marry him.

Tomorrow we film the caribou
Noogooshoweetok brought in,
tame as a grouse

At the Fruit-Tree's Mossy Root
(1968, 1980)

The Underground

Persephone
(if that was she)
taught the dull roots underground
(limp roots—drugged with frost and rock)
taught them myths of light of day
herded them like flocks of sheep
piped to them of running brooks
sighed to them of fragrant breeze
whispered tales of growing green.

She talked of shoots
to those pale roots ending just above her head;
tendrils on the passage walls
roots that lined Dis's treasure halls
Roots that slept both night and night
Bored with darkness after dark.

Chaffing fingers as she talked,
she rent their sleep
with dreams: of wheat
waving in the sun, of air,
moonlight, space, soft fields; of dew,
balmy showers, flowers, corn
tasseled, plumed grain, leaves uncurled;
ferns unrolled, trees unfurled;
green of a mallard's neck, thin green
of a grasshopper's wing, of
evergreen shoots, mossy stones;
singing of her home where frogs
chorused in the marsh behind
the hill, singing of all that
warm, moist, soft, green spaciousness
she recalled from the surface.

Variation underground
never caught her eye—the blacks,
silvers, wan grays—a dreadful
spectrum like the slick, upturned
belly of dead fish or snake.

Orphic song inspired the roots.
Persephone, if that was she
who wept to sing,
had taught them spring.

Peas

Sitting on the screened porch,
cane seat cool against backs
of hot knees,
the crisp crack of green dorsal lines
under thumb,
and the low spreading thunder
of peas
into big aluminum pans.

Voice Lessons

For Addie Richardson Fox (1862-1945)

I Under the Forsythia Bush

Have I ever been small?
Me is not small; me, me?
Me has no size,
cannot hide in a mouse's hole,
in a cow's stomach . . . .
(Though I remember my secret perfumed cave
under spring's forsythia bush—
its dome of beaten gold,
the red brick I sat on;
my kingdom of asparagus fern,
dusty green lace against blue silk.)
The cave, my kingdom were small,
of course, but I?
Of course not.

Me has no size.
Is inviolable, beyond dimension.

The voice lessons I do not remember.
I am told.

I am told Great Grandmother carried me
about the house and yard, an hour a day,
giving me what she called "voice lessons"—
croonings and sillinesses
and scales
and paddlings of hands.

When I walked, we walked:
up the quiet country road to visit neighbors;
We went to town in the car.
I do not remember, really,
but they tell me so.

All I can see now is her photograph;
she stands among bushes.
dark they are, like her severe dress,
severe like her face,
like the musty covers of her methods books
in the attic's peeling trunks.

II Up in the Cherry Tree

One year, before the beetle-brown scabs fell
from the eyes of the French pussy willow,
she died.
I remember,
and they tell me so.
Words rise in me like sap in the maple.
They are her words.

Her I know not,
yet she grows more important,
her "Voice Lessons" more important.
They swept over me
like green spring gusts
that balloon the netting on a car-bed,
set on a screened porch for naps.

When the windbreak burned,
she carried me in her arms
through the house,
back and forth from end to ell.
She matched her step to mine,
her hand to mine.

She would climb the cherry tree
by the outhouse
and eat until she could no more.
"To outwit the crows," she said.
(I do not remember but am told.)

The Voice Lessons I do not recall.
Yet sit I here,
paddling my hands against keys,
singing
in no dimension.

Laurel

Laurel kneels in the kitchen,
next the woodbox.
Above her neat gray head
hang the aebleskive
and the corn stick pan,
steel-wooled into mat black decorum,
the distelfink trivet
and the iron matchbox.
She hunkers down in her own glow,
her brass patella's
(engraved, rococo)
warm as cocoa
in December.

In the dark woodshed
splitting apple and oak and pine
we think of you,
of you, Laurel—
amid the perfumes of cold soil,
wet pitch, crushed cones.
Frost ferns coil
on the small window panes.
Frost pinwheels whirl
on the ends of logs:
crystal calendars.

Sometimes we lift off one breast
and pop in potato peels—
to burn the creosote
in your throat.

Sometimes we toss in horse chestnuts,
to detonate against your belly.
(We laugh like cob jelly.)

Oh Laurel,
how we love your bread, buns,
flapjacks, bacon, Sally Lunn,
sausage, coffee and grits.
Cakes rise in your bowls
as angels rise to God.
To you we usher in our friends,
draping their wet mittens on the wood box
to steam.
We share,
O comrade.

The Barn in Winter

(Even now the fug of manure is home—
warm and companionable.)
I cross the barnyard head drawn in,
gravel not iced down nipping my shins,
and the dead click of the frosted latch
admits me to a warmer realm,
where red and white space heaters steam:

Shuffling in place,
pressing down levers in water bowls
that allow drink to gush;
moist tongues hunting down the last husks
of grain or orange peel
or molasses-drizzled silage,
or reeling in strands of hay like pasta.
Their tongues wear shallow dishes in the concrete
fronting their stanchions,
the stanchions themselves polished as fine chairs
from years of attention with hairy cloths.

Under coquettish lashes
their liquid eyes
turn and dote upon me,
hoping for more grain or syrup.
The freshly whitewashed stone foundations
dream like clouds
above the red hills of warm flanks;
sawdust sings down the chutes from the upper floor;
the steers bawl;
the bull sneezes into his nose ring;
the milking machines chuff and chug;
the mouser waits for her milk.

Overwhelming as ether,
this cave and its inhabitants;
my senses labor like the water pump
to keep pace.

Auras, Tendrils (1984)

Entering the Surroundings

Entering the surroundings
one does not speak.
One enters into the chickadee
eating alder seeds
upside down
and into the dry crunch of snow underfoot.
Enters into the cold,
the dogs' howls echoing from the ravine
where water dreams and thrashes its legs
under ice.
Loses one's self entering.
Enters one's self.

Masks

Under the salty, weathered surface
the wood is soft, shines—
viscera.
My curved knife sinks in sweetly.

When I am not sure
how deep to cut—
above the chin,
under the brow ridge—
my fingers automatically
measure my own face,
my damp brow.

Thus the wolf
and the bad shaman
come to look familiar,
like brothers—
as they should.

Auras, Tendrils

New Year's we heaved
the tree out on the white garden,
to wait spring
and brush-burning.
Storms draped its tinsel
everywhere.

In May more than silvered plastic
glints on the seeded earth,
the border of viburnum,
the birch green belt and gravel paths.
Auras attract these visible signs,
these clutching fingers.

The turgid seed
thrusts out its green phallus
under a silver transmitter.
Our hands on the hoe
send out fans (like lichen or coral),
heat and non-heat,
silver streamers
hoping to catch (like bean tendrils)
at a rough sensor somewhere.
The spruce emits a spruce-shape
Plato would find ideal.

Tinsel flares peripherally,
making its turn;
every 90 minutes,
tendrils.

In Velvet

An Athapaskan Indian girl, in a winter village in Interior Alaska before 1800, muses on her puberty confinement.

When I hear the gravel rattling in the basket lid,
then I know the uncles are home from the trail,
and have turned to their carving
before the coals are cast out and the curtain drawn,
before they bed down in the kashim.
They are making masks for my Woman's Feast,
and each shall be different.
Some will be like the enemies-beyond-the-mountain.
Some will have fierce beards of bear hide.
Some will be feathered like the raven.
Some will have spirit's teeth,
as if to eat me.
(These will frighten the youngest.)
No one speaks of me,
but the rattles speak.

Here they have painted a bee
on the matting,
and this is to remind me
of the spring,
when honeybees migrate,
and the old queen takes half the colony in a swarm
to a birch.
Scouts fly from the birch seeking a new camp,
one that will keep them warm and dry
during the dark time.
When a camp is chosen, the swarm goes there.

And here they have carved a bee,
yellow cedar from the south,
with ivory wings
and baleen eyes,
and hung it by a length of sinew
from the rafters.
And this is to remind me when I am a woman
I will never rest.
And to be thankful for this seclusion.
For the bee never rests,
but is always seeking wildflowers as we seek marten-skins.

Many beautiful things are here in the shadows with me,
my drinking tube and grease bag
are more beautiful than any things I had before;
the swan's leg bone is polished,
and the bag is sewn with porcupine quills, red and blue.
These charm me into the future,
where I must be wife, and mother.

The old women whisper of pain, and of pleasure, too.
I fear both.
All I know of pleasure is the swans down on the strap
of my grease bag.

When the shaman dons his mask
with the two eyes, one copper,
the other blue abalone shell,
and the raven feathers behind,
when he is burned and returns in the morning,
when he twirls,
and all blurs,
copper and shell and light on the river,
and you begin falling into the blur....

Here I am falling
and when all begins to blur,
bee and matting,
I reach for my pail quickly, quickly, quickly,
and sip through the swan tube,
and then smear my lips with grease
to ease my hunger.

It is hard to hear them about their work:
taking the curtain off the smoke hole
and making the fire,
the hiss of hot rocks in the birch meat pot,
the smell of boiling muskrat,
the rustle of fish-skin parkas
as they take them out and slip through the door.
I hear them singing at the cache,
the young girls carrying water from the river.

I imagine the spoon of horn from the south
that mother uses to dish up hot meat;
the face on the horn handle
seems to flicker on the matting,
laughing at me,
the unfinished woman.

It is hard to sit here
month and month, cold,
cold food only,
grass anklets making my shins itch,
beaded mittens covering my hands—
I am not to scratch or touch.

I am twelve winters, a despised female,
my grandmother and aunts whisper when
they bring my dry fish;
they whisper I am lucky
that my nose was not stopped with moss
and I left to die at birth in the forest.
It was a good summer for *oolachen*,
so they kept me, a despised female,
and the oil ran down my fat chin.

I am permitted to remove these mittens at evening,
to go outside, my hood shading my face,
on the separate trail, to wash my face
and comb my hair. It is hard to return.

I am as one dead to the world—

or buried alive, stones at my sides,
listening to life outside my stones.

I cannot touch my food;
water cannot touch my lips except
through this swan's-bone.
I press the beading on my moose-hide mittens
against my cold cheeks,
press and scrape
to see if I can still feel.

I helped to plait these walls of grass,
walls that closet me now--
not knowing.
Some girls run off (the ones-who-will-not-marry)—

but they are in disgrace if found;
devoured by Silver-Tip if not found—

or made slaves by those not our kin.

Now they are eating ice-cream,
chewing mouse-food
that I myself stole from mouse-holes.
I hear the rattle of deer teeth
sewn into my brother's trousers.
Small brother, the tail of his fox cap drags behind.
His lips are shiny with the best fat;
he is plump with kisses,
and wanders in and out of the *kashim*
like a whiskered seal.

Smoke, stale air.
A whiff of the warm forest
comes to me, the scene of the grassy places
where dewberries hide.
Smoke, smoke, smoke.

But I shall not cry.
I shall not cry when I am wed,
or refuse the husband they choose,
or pour dirty water in his alder cup.
My breasts flourish like these chevrons of beads,
red and pointed,
soft as cottonwood down, as eider bellies.
(I shall please my husband,
and he shall bring home fine skins to sew.)

I hear small brother playing in the pile of deer bones,
the pile of moose racks, of fish bones,
of mussel shells.
All the piles he rifles;
he drums, the "little chief."

No one speaks of me.
I have not been immodest.
I am pure.
Why do they not miss me?
Am I so worthless?
Do they fear my new power,
the might of the red clay they paint on the skulls
at Ancestor Feast?

Ice formed on my hair when they washed it,
and then quickly, quickly, quickly,
they cast me inside this closet,
mother only whispering a few words:
that I must no longer be seen until married,
that I am no longer a child because of this redness.
They pulled this new hood (my velvet) on me;
the ice beneath melted down my back.
I must stay, grandmother says,
until the end of next salmon season,
through the time of darkness,
and the time of birds' eggs, the time of Fireweed greens,
the time of lighted nights.
Auntie says to be thankful I am not a princess,
for then I would stay here longer.

When the red runs, I dream of slippery fish,
slipping down my thighs to our nets.
I dream of the crooked salmon,
fish, fish, fish.

Canoeing in the Rain (1990)

Into the Realm of the Seal

When the world was new,
when the land had just risen, steaming, from the waves,
when red and black clinkers still slunk forward, clanking,
into cold waves,
there was a time before man,
before Anangula,
before Chaluka,
before Bering and Pribylov,
before grass mats,
before sod roofs,
before fine baskets and sleek baidarkas,
before Hrdlicka,
before relocation.

It was before the first woman emerged from a volcano's crater
and gave birth on black sand;
before her children clung to the broad backs of cormorants
and were whisked to all corners of the world.

It was a time before masks,
before The Dry Ones sat content in their caves,
before whaling,
before tattoos and feast bowls,
before fishing spears and kamleikas.

It was the realm of the seal,
when everything slippery throve in the waves—
devilfish, black fish, whales and cod.
It was a time before flippers dreamed of feet.

If we could imagine that time,
before quotas and schools and books,
before guns and rye bread,
before steamboats and clocks,
before whistles and six-packs,
we would sing of it.

But it is hard to go back now into that realm.
The villages are dying,
and the names of islands slip away on the tide
like fingerlings.
It is hard to sing
of the realm of the seal.

Aleut Lullaby

Looking over my shoulder with your black eyes,
you watch me crimping boot soles in my teeth.
Looking over my shoulder,
you watch me cooking dog food,
watch the howling dogs strain at their ropes.
Looking over my shoulder.
you see me scouring pots,
plucking puffins.

You are welcome as eggs,
welcome as berries,
welcome as whales in spring,
my son.
I feel your cold toes on my back.
They are little cold stars.

Before you came I was full, too full,
stretched and frightened.
Now I am myself again,
and I carry you into the world.
Bashful, you sleep.
When I told my little sister about you,
she tried to lift my parka.
"Show me!" she pleaded.
"I want to see him."
She did not understand.
It was hard to explain you were still in my seal poke;
you were not yet born.
I was afraid to cross open water on steppingstones of ice,
afraid I would fall and harm you.

Do not frown at uncles over my shoulder.
Do not cry in alarm.
We all work together in our village.
We are all relatives; we all feed one another.

I lick you clean; I rub you down with old furs.
I diaper you in moss and skins.
Oh, large-eyed seal,
sleep out of the wind.
Wake and drink.
Then stand on eager tiptoe and peer over my shoulder.
See the world. See the open water.
See the table set when the tide goes out.

You are welcome as murre eggs,
welcome as sea urchins.
I show you to my small sister.
"Oh see his pretty large eyes," she says.
She snugs you into her own parka back.
Your cold toes are little stars on her dark skin.
I sing you this lullaby.

How Little Children Come to Suffer

To Max, on his eighth birthday, Mother's Day, May 11, 1986

Dear Max.
I haven't met you, but you kept me awake last night—
your cigarette-burned chest,
The vicious scar above your left ankle.
In the video I saw, the one made on Good Friday,
with everyone coloring eggs,
Your foster father asks how you feel about being Athabascan.
"I'm only part Indian," you say;
"When people know I'm Indian, they tell me to go away."
You hunch thin shoulders closer to your bony chest.

"What makes you happy?"
he asks.
"Doing things I like," he says.
"What makes you sad?"
You shrug your shoulders, your beautiful face is so mournful.

The kids from the villages have a game.
It's called "Parent falling down drunk."
They do it to perfection—
the slurred speech,
the unbalanced gait,
the slide to the floor.
You have no table manners.
You shovel Chinese food into your mouth at plate level.
"Mom didn't always make dinner," you explain.
"She was sick."

The kids from the villages have a game.
they do it to perfection—the snoring, the incoherent mumbling,
the running to the honey bucket to vomit.
They have no table manners.
They eat quickly and efficiently.
Not a grain of fried rice falls to the floor.

The kids from the villages have a game.
Ask them about their scars
and they say, "When people get drunk,
they throw rocks at me."
They pull socks up quickly
And sleeves way down;
they button everything up to the neck,
tuck their ankles under them
and go on drawing pictures of families with two parents.
The kids from the villages
are good little mimics,
whirling and falling down.
If you bring a six-pack into the house,
they blow up.
They are sure someone will fall down;
there will be no dinner;
the baby will cry.
This is how the little children
come to suffer.

Dear Max,
What can I say to you when I meet you Saturday?
You don't like to be hugged;
you don't like to be touched.
You hate women.
You dream about speed boats and Hollywood
and a Daddy whose back you can ride on,
a Daddy you can talk about at Show and Tell.

Women aren't to be trusted.
They change their minds.
They put you in state custody for little vacations
while they dry out.
Then they take you back.
They don't like you,
because they've been beaten by others of your sex.
Mothers only fall down, and vomit,
and forget you're hungry,
and tell you to lock yourself in the bathroom
before they get violent, before they throw hairbrushes and rocks.
This is how the little children come to suffer.
This is the game in the villages, the suburbs, the cities.

Dear Max,
When I meet you in three days,
what can I say?
What can anyone say?

Side Spike

Eleven now,
Max may choose his own hairstyle.
He chooses the side-spike–
a punk look
in which the right side stands straight out from the skull.
It looks like half a bentwood hat,
the conical Aleut warrior's helmet
decorated with sea lion whiskers and glyphs;
the magnificent visor the baidarka navigator
wore in open water
to shield his eyes from the glare;
a hat with the shape of unnamed volcanoes,
unnumbered waves.

Out in your new hat, son,
don't forget your sea lion floats,
the inflated bladders
tied to kelp ropes
tied to stone anchors.
Remember to let them down to mark your way home.

Meanwhile, mousse slick as wet seal gut
keeps the shape of the side spike
just right
for that next voyage
into the unknown.

The Octopus: An Essay

Ann Fox Chandonnet

©Yvonne Mozée

I

Flopsy, Mopsy, and Me

Beatrix Potter spoke to my soul. As a small child I went around muttering under my breath, "Flopsy, Mopsy, Cottontail and Peter."

As an adult, analyzing this, I call it "an interrupted series" or a "variegated series." Under normal circumstances, that phrase should have been Flopsy, Mopsy, Dropsy and Bopsy. But from the bottom of my discriminating little brain, I objected to that order. My poetry—and even some of my prose—has frequently made use of this verbal structure.

While muttering, I was collecting "pretty rocks." My pockets were always full. They were something I could "own," inspect, admire. My pretty rocks annoyed my mother no end, because they wound up in the washing machine.

At some point I surrendered pebbles and began collecting birds' nests and the splintery wooden boxes that salted cod came in.

II

My Great-Grandmother

One of the chief influences toward my future in literature came from my Great-Grandmother. She began my dive into the sea of words by talking to me daily for an hour. I enjoyed nearly two years of that blessing, which I thoroughly believe made me, me. Words, phrases seemed as palpable as granite outcroppings—objects to grasp between thumb and pincher.

Part of my extended Dracut household, GG had earlier in life been a matron at a school for the deaf. At the Old Yellow Meeting House, she was admired as a talented Sunday school teacher. Sixty years later, at a meeting of the Dracut Historical Society, one of her students recalled, to my delight, the felt story boards she used to illustrate Bible tales.

When I was born early in 1943, Great-Gram began carrying me (or walking with me) every day for an hour. These times she called "Voice Lessons."

My-Great Gram left the farm two weeks before my second birthday. Colon cancer. She died at home as most people did then. I remember clearly being ushered into her bedroom to say goodbye. Of course, I did not understand death except for associating it with Red Riding Hood's wolves.

III

Bookworm

In my single-digit years, I didn't know that such a thing as a library existed, until one day when my elementary class paraded to the nearby Dracut Public Library. Soon I wanted to move in. I was devastated when I learned that the Bobbsey Twins series contained only thirteen volumes!

Fortunately, the farmhouse attic stocked best-sellers from the 20s: *The Secret Garden* and the Oz series, for example, as well as *China to Me*, *We* and *Kon-Tiki*. I read the same books over and over and dreamed of great adventures. *Readers' Digest Condensed Books* introduced me to topics like Andersonville, puerperal fever, and cerebral palsy. For my ninth birthday Gram gave me the heavily illustrated *National Geographic* volume about Ancient Egyptians; I was hooked on ancient peoples.

IV

Places

Home for my first twenty-one years was a 180-acre apple farm in Dracut. I say, "I grew up . . ." with the same passion that I tell people, "I lived thirty-four years in Alaska."

On the one hand, the farm was a paradise. It gave me freedom to wander in quiet thickets, cathedral-like glades; to enjoy ponds with tadpoles and goldfish, natural springs, blueberry bushes—without company or ruckus. When I say that I grew up on a Dracut apple and dairy farm, it has the same evocative resonance for me as "I had a farm in Africa, at the foot of the Ngong Hills." It was a blessing comparable to Walden Pond.

On the other hand, I was teased with "bookworm." There was little encouragement for my love affair with words, and in my early double-digit years it was hard to find a blank sheet of paper. But I was stubborn.

V

A Declaration

For some literary artists, a series of discrete events carries them into the realm of writing. I can name two: attending a high school performance of *The Mikado*; seeing an early TV performance of *Cyrano de Bergerac*.

By age sixteen, I was so wound up over the world of words that I made a declaration: I would be a serious poet for life. I have never surrendered that goal.

VI

A Second Paradise

Alaska became my second paradise. I dove right in, experiencing the state through hiking, camping, canoeing, kayaking, swimming with loons, and (in honor of our thirtieth anniversary) snowshoeing from the top of Chilkoot Pass. Thirty-four years in Alaska brimmed with sheer delight; I particularly loved introducing my sons to Nature.

Over the decades, my themes continue to be the same: places, people, revelations, experiences, celebrations, intuitions, discoveries. I believe in "writing what you don't know," so research comes into play, as in "In the Horse" and "In Velvet."

VII

The Octopus

Attempting to write this essay, I have produced four versions. It is an octopus with too many legs.

Writing is a form of translation, from the language of thought to the language of words. Techniques can be taught, but talent cannot. My writing birthed from the influence of nursery rhymes, hymns, popular tunes—almost anything that entered at eye or ear. My brain craves this food as a thirsty person yearns for water; passionately, with every sinew. There is a necessity to it that may not register with others; devotion to the literary arts may seem foolish, insignificant. But here I am, entangled.

Notes

NEW

“Snow Water under Culverts”: *Mayflowers*: state flower of Massachusetts.

“The Civil War Ink Bottle: Minie ball: after C. E. Minie (1814-79), French inventor of a cone-shaped bullet popular in the 19th century.” *Contraband*: A term invented by Gen. Benjamin Butler of Lowell to describe slaves smuggled or found behind Union lies. *Dead Line*: A largely unmarked margin around the edge of Andersonville; Union prisoners who ventured into this border were shot. Now associated with newspapers. *Andersonville*: a notorious prison in Georgia.

“Fine Shining Weather”: *Ahwahneechee*: Original Native Americans in Yosemite; derived from their name for the site, Ahwahnee, “gaping-mouth-like place.” *George Catlin*: American adventurer and painter who specialized in portraits of Native Americans created during five trips to the American West in the 1830s. *Mendota*: A lake in Madison, Wisc.

“Iris Is Last”: *Shem Pete*, a noted elder of the Denaina, the Athabascan Indians of Cook Inlet. *K’tilla*: a wild plant found in damp places. *Beaded soles*: moccasins for the dead.

“Learning Eskimo Dancing/Lighting up the World”: Compare Eskimo arm movements and dance scenes with the Hawaiian huk-e-lau, in which a nest is cast out and many fish pulled in.

“Sitka”: *Petroglyphs:* prehistoric markings etched into stone. *Labret*: a protruding facial decoration consisting of a plate inserted below the lower lip. *Katlian*: Name of a Tlingit chief; also the name off a bay where seaweed is traditionally gathered on tidal flats. *Baranof/Baranov*: Alexander Andreyevich (1747-1819). Russian explorer, fur trader; governor of Russian Alaska. Ivan *Veniaminov*: linguist, missionary priest in Alaska; later St. Innocent of Alaska. *Gajaa Heen*: Heen means river; name of a village founded by Baranof in 1789, seven miles north of Sitka. Today, the name of a Sitka dance group which performs in authentic regalia. *Kiksadi*: One of the largest and most revered clans of the Tlingit Raven moiety.

"Cogs Within Cogs": *Berners Bay*, a wilderness area north of Juneau accessible only by boat. *Hermit Street*: A short street above the old Juneau cemetery; my address.

"It Pushes": Imagines a prehistoric event on the ocean shore at Barrow. *Ivu/ivoo*: Eskimo word for a fierce winter windstorm which pushes ice cakes from the sea surface onto the shore with no warning.
Barrow: An Inupiaq village on Alaska's North Slope.

"Under Mendenhall": *Mendenhall*: one of the largest retreating glaciers on the outskirts of Juneau. *Cornell Box*: A shadow-box-like art form invented by Joseph Cornell; he called them
"poetic theaters" or "memories."

"Brash Ice": *Tongass*: nation's largest national forest; covers most of Southeast Alaska; embraces Juneau on its inland side.

"See and Release": *Susitna*: a river north of Anchorage.

"Words for Shadows": An oil supertanker, the Exxon *Valdez*, struck rocks while leaving port and created an oil spill that covered 460 square miles; March 24, 1989. *Sea otters*: marine mammals with luscious fur; using forced Aleut ad Athabascan labor, the Russians harvested them until the 1810s, by which time they had decimated the population. Baranof was one of the culprits. The spill killed approximately: 250,000 seabirds (such as cormorants), 3,000 otters, 250 bald eagles, 300 seals and 22 killer whales.

"Circle of Stones": *Big Times*: end-of-the-year festivities allowed to slaves in the American South. For one day, slaves were free of work, given extra food, and sometimes lengths of fabric.

"Borning Room": A room in John Greenleaf Whittier's birthplace in Haverhill, Massachusetts.

"The Final Approach": *North Tower*, one of the Twin Towers destroyed on Sept. 11, 2001.

"The Hare in Tuckerman's Ravine": *Tuckerman's* is one of the main trail approaches to Mt. Washington (Presidential Range, New Hampshire).

"Willendorf, Early June": *The Venus of Willendorf* (30,000 years old) is perhaps the most aesthetically pleasing of dozens of Venuses created in Austria and parts of France where caves are common. It is also one of the most complete. Formerly, authorities thought these figures were playthings for me; but recently they have been found on unmistakable altars. *Eagle*, etc.: Bird bones suited for caving flutes/whistles were found in *Stone, Bone, Antler & Shell: Artifacts of the Northwest Coast*, Hilary Stewart (1996 edition).

"Peavey, A Letter": *Peavey*: a heavy wooden tool with a pointed metal tip and a hinged hook; used to shift logs.

"Whalescape": *Flense*r: one who dissects whale blubber using a blade on a long handle.

"September 15, 12:04 p.m.": *Chugiak*, an Athabascan Indian term meaning "place of many places." Also spelled "Chugach."

"Maui"*: Maui*: one of the Hawaiian Islands. *Winslow Homer*, an American painter.

"Mary Porter is Carried from the Morning Star Baptist Church in Mattapan": *Mattapan*, an area of Greater Boston.

SELECTED

"Love in Motherlode Country": *Tincup, Fairplay*, etc., California Gold Rush towns; now mostly deserted.

"The Island": *Henry Gemmill*, editor of the *National Observer* (d. 1994). *Abbie Hoffman*: American social activist (1936-1989) who co-founded the Youth International Party. *Jean Shepard*: known for film *The Christmas Story*; *Sanche de Gramont*: AKA Ted Morgan, American biographer (born 1932).

"Van Cliburn Among the Crowberries": *Van Cliburn*: A concert pianist of the 20th century. *Mastaba*: bread loaf-shaped Egyptian tomb. Straight sides lean in to the narrower top. Typically, the tomb of a lesser government official.

"Sonatina, Inukshuk": *Inukshuk*, a human figure of piled rocks, used to herd caribou and mark tundra property lines. *Oogruk*: bearded seal.

"Woods (Lowell)": James *Whistler*: Lowell-born artist who spent much of his adulthood in Europe.

"On a Human Scale": *Ninilchik*: An Athabascan village on the Kenai Peninsula.

"Entering the Surroundings": This poem was adopted as the Processional for *A Mass for Winter Solstice* (University of Alaska, Fairbanks).

"In Velvet": A stage of a male moose's antlers during annual re-growth from scratch. As the antlers grow, they are protected by a vascular "felt-like" substance. The scholarly notes to this poem may be found in *Auras, Tendrils*.

"Into the Realm of the Seal": *Anangula*: an Aleutian Paleo-Arctic site rich in deposits of prehistoric microblades. *Chaluka*: A prehistoric archaeological site and National Historic Landmark at Nikolski,, on Unmak Island, Aleutians. Believed to have been for 4000 years or so continuously occupied. *Vitus Bering*: navigator and explorer in the service of Russia; d. 1741. *Pribylov*: A Russian sea captain, c. 1786; a group of islands he "discovered." *Baidarka*: An Eskimo/Inuit boat with a driftwood frame; larger than a kayak. *Hrdlicka*: an anthropologist (1869-1943), born in Czechoslovakia, moved to the United States and became one of the first proponents of the theory that Native Americans arrived via the Bering Land Bridge.

A Note on the Author

The oldest of five children, Ann Fox Chandonnet was born in Lowell, Mass., growing up in the neighboring rural town of Dracut. She attended Lowell State College (as it was then) as an English major/history minor, class of 1964, graduating magna cum laude. She earned a master's degree in English at the University of Wisconsin (Madison), and then accepted a position as an English teacher at Kodiak High School in Alaska. After a year on Kodiak Island, she returned to Lowell and became a teaching assistant at Lowell State for three years.

In 1969 she and her husband, Fernand L. Chandonnet, moved to Oakland, Calif., where she learned banking at one bank and then was hired away by a second, First Enterprise Bank, the first Black-owned bank in the city, to be administrative assistant to the President. She also published her first cookbook, *The Complete Fruit Cookbook* (101 Productions, San Francisco).

The couple adopted their first child, Yves Gaetan, ten days old, in Costa Rica in 1972. Fern was hired by radio station KHAR in Anchorage to be its "morning man" (a combination news reader and comedian) in 1973.

In 1974, they adopted their second son, Alexandre Jules. Ann remained at home for ten years to raise the boys while carving out time for words. She then spent ten years as a reporter for the *Anchorage Times*, moving in 1999 to Juneau to work for the Juneau *Empire*.

Among her honors is an award from The Alaska Press Club for a seven-part series, "Disabled by Alcohol Before Birth." Her long poem "In Velvet" was twice nominated for the Pushcart Prize.

Her latest book is a children's book, *Baby Abe: A Lullaby for Lincoln* (Circles Press, 2021).